D0606462

Robert de La Salle

SAMUEL WILLARD CROMPTON

GREAT EXPLORERS

Jacques Cartier

James Cook

Hernán Cortés

Sir Francis Drake

Vasco da Gama

Sir Edmund Hillary

Robert de La Salle

Lewis and Clark

Ferdinand Magellan

Sir Ernest Shackleton

GREAT EXPLORERS

Robert de La Salle

SAMUEL WILLARD CROMPTON

CHELSEA HOUSE
PUBLISHERS
An imprint of Infobase Publishing

GREAT EXPLORERS: ROBERT DE LA SALLE

Chelsea House
An imprint of Infobase Publishing
132 West 31st Street
New York, NY 10001

Library of Congress Cataloging-in-Publication Data
Crompton, Samuel Willard.
  Robert de La Salle / Samuel Willard Crompton.
    p. cm. — (Great explorers)
  Includes bibliographical references and index.
  ISBN 978-1-60413-419-3 (hardcover)
  1. La Salle, Robert Cavelier, sieur de, 1643–1687—Juvenile literature.
2. Explorers—North America—Biography—Juvenile literature. 3. Explorers
—Canada—Biography—Juvenile literature. 4. Mississippi River Valley—
Discovery and exploration—French—Juvenile literature. I. Title. II. Series.
  F1030.5.C886 2009
  977'.01092—dc22
  [B]
                2009014166

Series design by Lina Farinella
Cover design by Keith Trego

Printed in the United States of America

Bang EJB 10 9 8 7 6 5 4 3 2 1

This book is printed on acid-free paper.

All links and Web addresses were checked and verified to be correct at the time of publication. Because of the dynamic nature of the Web, some addresses and links may have changed since publication and may no longer be valid.

CONTENTS

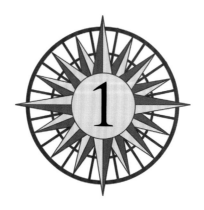

Seven
Feet Under

ON JULY 13, 1995, UNDERWATER DIVERS WORKING FOR THE Texas Historical Commission made one of the most sensational archaeological finds of modern times. Diving off a ship platform in the southern part of Texas's Matagorda Bay, the divers came upon the wreck of what was clearly a seventeenth- or eighteenth-century ship. They knew this from the angle of the craft, and from the kind of timbers used. To their astonishment, the divers found the wreck in only seven feet of water but covered with silt which had preserved the wreck over the past three centuries.

Identification

The divers, and the archaeologists to whom they handed pieces of wood, copper, and iron, hoped that this would be the fulfillment of a dream of many years. They hoped they had located the oldest French shipwreck found in the New World.

Unfortunately, they could not make a positive identification for days—weeks, in fact—because the measurements they took had to be checked and compared with those of the original architect for the ship and those records were found only in France.

Weeks passed before the divers announced that the wreck was 51-foot (15.5 meters) long, and that she bore markings which suggested she came from France. Weeks later, in the archives of the French navy, a document was found, referring to the *Belle*, a 51-foot-long bark (*barque longue*) built in 1684, especially for the expedition of Robert Cavelier de La Salle. This is what the divers and archaeologists had hoped for.

Coffer-Dam

The leaders of the Texas Historical Commission decided that this would be one of the greatest archaeological works of their time, and that they had to get it right. Over the next few months, a coffer-dam (two concentric rectangles of steel) was built around the wreck of the *Belle*, and, over a three-day period, all the water in that area was laboriously pumped out. There, on the bottom of Matagorda Bay, lay the wreck of a ship built in 1684 and wrecked in 1686.

The *Belle* was in remarkably good condition. The silt of the bay had denied oxygen to the timbers of the wreck, helping to preserve the wood from decay. The hull of the 51-foot-long vessel lay there on the floor of the bay, and archaeologists went to work to identify and remove the artifacts preserved since the time of King Louis XIV.

The Remains

Rope, several thousand feet of it, was found, coiled in exactly the way it had been done in the naval ports of France. Tightly packed jars revealed their treasures—beads, glass, mirrors, and paint— all designed for trade with Native Americans. The remains of

The sinking of the last of La Salle's four ships, the *Belle*, in 1686, left the settlers stranded on the Texas coast, with no hope of rescue. For over three centuries the wreckage lay forgotten until 1995 when a team of archaeologists from the Texas Historical Commission recovered the entire shipwreck and over a million artifacts. Pictured, salvage workers stand on the deck of the cofferdam built around the shipwreck of the *Belle*.

cockroaches and rats were also found, suggesting that the *Belle* was not a healthy ship, at least by modern-day standards.

The archaeologists used wet vacs (short for *vacuum*) to remove debris, until they found precious artifacts like a cobbler's tool. They found more destructive devices too, including a set of "fire pots," or buckets containing explosives and shrapnel, which would have been used if a pirate ship had come alongside. Hundreds of brass rings were discovered, but the truly big finds were the six cannon of the ship. Hoisted out, one by one, they formed a key part of the collections of the Texas Historical

Commission, tangible evidence of the commitment Louis XIV had made to La Salle and his dream of colonization in Texas. The finding of the *Belle* confirmed what some scholars had long suspected: that the attempt to colonize the mouth of the Mississippi was a major undertaking, with significant assistance from the French crown.

One Man

Near the ship's bow, the archaeologists found the skeleton of a man, who had, presumably, rushed to the bow to prevent from sinking with his ship. His hopes for survival dashed, he had gone down with the *Belle*.

Archaeologists and forensic scientists employed the very latest techniques to reconstruct what this man would have looked like. His skeletal remains suggest he was over 40 years old, and was therefore probably a colonist rather than a sailor (sailors tended to be in their teens and twenties). Reconstruction resulted in a composite picture of a man, five-foot-four-inches (163 centimeters) tall, who possessed the large nose and expressive face typical of Frenchmen of that time. This human reconstruction was perhaps the most satisfying of all the work done by the Texas archaeologists, because they were able to put a human face onto the tragedy of La Salle's final voyage.

Almost two years after the wreck was found, the remains of the *Belle* were firmly sheltered within the holdings of the historical commission. The coffer-dam was removed, and the sea swept in to reclaim that tiny section which had been held back by man's ingenuity.

Finding the *Belle* answered a number of questions historians had puzzled over for years. For example, the wreck and its artifacts revealed:

> Louis XIV and his government sent all they could on this voyage.

La Salle and his men were confused about their location. Matagorda Bay was not an ideal place for them to begin their settlement.

Still, other questions remained:

How had La Salle made such a mistake in basic geography, landing in Texas rather than Louisiana?
Why had the captain of the *Belle* allowed his precious cargo to be wrecked?
Could the French have succeeded in their daring colonization project?

The Work Continues

Even the *Belle*, with something like one million artifacts, cannot provide all the answers. History was, and is, an unfolding process in which scholars working in quiet solitude contribute their best, and where divers and archaeologists sometimes hit the mother lode. Collaboration between the two sometimes leads to breakthroughs, and so it was with the finding of the *Belle*. Much more is known of La Salle and his ill-fated colony, but quite a bit remains to be discovered, perhaps by some lucky diver or some surprised farmer, working in his backyard.

A Norman in America

ROBERT CAVELIER DE LA SALLE WAS BORN IN ROUEN, Normandy, in northwestern France, in November 1643. He was baptized on November 22, and the parish record reports his full name as shown above. He gave himself the name Rene-Robert Cavelier, Sieur de La Salle sometime later in life.

La Salle's father, Jean Cavelier, was a prosperous merchant of Rouen, and the family owned a small estate just outside of the town. This "fief," as landholdings were called, was named La Salle, and this addition to the family name became the part best known to history. Robert Cavelier de La Salle is usually known as simply "La Salle," while his father is Jean Cavelier, and his elder brother carries that same name.

The People and the Province

La Salle and most of his fellow Normans were the descendants of Vikings (Norsemen) who had come south in the ninth century after Christ. The Northmen (people later converted this to

"Normans") came as conquerors, but they stayed because the land and its surrounding waters were so appealing. The famous monastery of Mont-St-Michel is in Normandy, and many older Americans today still have a special feeling for Normandy, because it is the place where American soldiers landed on June 6, 1944, in the operation known forever since as "D-Day."

By the eleventh century, the descendants of the Viking conquerors had become ardent Christians, eager to spread the faith and to win glory for themselves. In 1066, Duke William of Normandy crossed the English Channel (which separates England from northern France and serves as Great Britain's key natural defense against invading armies), attacked England, and won the Battle of Hastings, which determined that England would also have its share of Norman people, culture, and laws. Just 30 years later, when Pope Urban II called for the First Crusade against the Muslims in Jerusalem, Norman knights, earls, and barons made up a disproportionate number of the leaders of that military campaign. Normans also conquered the island kingdom of Sicily, just south of Italy, in the eleventh century. Some historians choose to call Normans the "supermen" of that period.

By the time La Salle was born, in 1643, the Normans were a good deal less warlike. They were superb merchants, mariners, and tradesmen, but they no longer dominated the ocean routes and the military campaigns of their time. Still, almost every young Norman was aware of a glorious heritage, and many, like La Salle, desired to further it through future adventures. It is safe to say that many Normans, even in La Salle's time, thought of themselves as Normans *first* and Frenchmen second.

With the Black Robes

Little is known of La Salle's early years, and the best one can do is imagine that he had the normal childhood of a middle-class Frenchman of the time. Letters written later in life indicated

Explorer Robert de La Salle traveled from France to Canada, exploring the regions of the Great Lakes. He developed relationships with several Native American groups and established several forts in Native American territory. Although he is now known for navigating the length of the Mississippi, his ultimate goal—to establish a colony at the mouth of the Mississippi—was unsuccessful.

he had a good education, from an early age, and that it was accelerated when he joined the Jesuit religious order (the Society of Jesus) around the age of 14.

The Jesuits had been founded by a Spaniard in the 1530s, and they were the most disciplined and adventuresome of all the religious orders of that time. Founded in order to combat the new Protestant heresies (for that is how Roman Catholics saw the beliefs of Martin Luther), the Jesuits became very involved in education and mission work. Many Jesuits volunteered to go on long, dangerous missions to foreign lands. One of the first Europeans to reach Japan was Saint Francis Xavier of the Jesuit order.

Jesuits were also among the first Frenchmen to go to Canada. The Native Americans of the Great Lakes, impressed with the character and strength of these priests, had labeled them "Black Robes." The name stuck.

La Salle may have joined the Jesuits with this kind of adventure in mind, but his superiors at the Jesuit schools found him something of a trial. In their records, these Jesuits acknowledge La Salle's fine mind and even hint at leadership abilities, but they also cite his disregard for the commands given by superiors.

His older brother, Jean Cavelier, had joined the Order of Saint Sulpice, and was doing well in that organization. By about 1665, Jean Cavelier had left France for Canada, to serve in the Sulpician Order in Montreal. La Salle had thoughts of joining his older brother in that far-off land.

New France

Canada, also called New France, had first been discovered by Jacques Cartier in 1535. More than half a century passed, however, before the French began to colonize, first in Quebec City and then Montreal. Around the time that La Salle began to think of Canada, a longtime settler there wrote to King Louis

XIV, explaining why it was so difficult to attract Frenchmen to come:

> It is true that there is something dreadful in the aspect of the approaches to this country called New France; for the sight of the Island of Newfoundland, on which is Placentia, of the Saint Pierre Islands, of Cape Ray, of Saint Paul's island, and of the mainland at the entrance of the Gulf [of Saint Lawrence] inspires dismay and an inclination to keep away.

There, in a nutshell, was the problem. Settlers coming from the Old World saw the rocks and bleak aspect of the land at the entrance of the St. Lawrence River. Many turned back at that point, and even those who continued on kept a painful memory of that frightening sight.

It is true that the landscape became—and becomes—much more hospitable as one progressed. The St. Lawrence River narrows as one travels up to Quebec City, and the barren rock and stone slowly give way to sandy soil in an area sculpted by the glaciers thousands of years ago. Still, all the efforts of Louis XIV and the French government did not persuade many Frenchmen and women to emigrate to America; in 1665, there were only about 4,000 people in the entire colony of New France.

Two years later, in 1667, La Salle sailed for America. He had asked permission to leave the Jesuit order (he had never taken final vows) and his superiors seemed delighted with this turn of events. La Salle toyed with the idea of going to the Caribbean, or perhaps South America, but in the end he decided on New France.

La Salle landed in Quebec in the autumn of 1667 and quickly went upriver to Montreal. He was impressed with the majestic beauty of Quebec and with the landscape that presented itself as he went to Montreal. Winters were long and summers were often uncomfortably hot, but Canada had much to offer an ambitious young man. There was wood and water everywhere, and an abundance of wild game to be hunted. Most of all there was the fur trade, which had become the temptation of many young Frenchmen.

No one knows if La Salle came with the beaver trade in mind, but within a year of his arrival the young Norman entered the business. At first he lived in Montreal, and stayed in good contact with his older brother. Doubtless it was through the efforts of his brother Jean, a Sulpician priest, that La Salle received a "fief," or landholding, from the brothers of Saint Sulpice. Located about eight miles (12.8 kilometers) southeast of Montreal, this new fief made La Salle a landowner of some

BEAVERS AND THEIR FUR

No one knows which European took the first puff of tobacco, a decision that led to the success of the Virginia colony. Likewise, no one knows which Frenchman, or perhaps Dutchman, first took a beaver skin and made it into a winter hat, but the industrious beaver proved to be the reason that many Europeans went to New France and New York.

The French arrived in Quebec in 1608, and the Dutch began to settle what is now Manhattan around 1626. Both peoples came in small numbers, at first, and they found no "cash" crop akin to tobacco. Within a decade of their arrival, however, the two Europeans peoples discovered a ready market for beaver furs in their homelands. The Dutch turned pelts into hats and coats and sold them to other people around Europe, while the French concentrated on internal consumption, meaning that every French nobleman wanted a fur cap and every French lady a fur coat.

The trade in beaver fur peaked in the 1640s, a time when the French court was almost littered with animal fur from the New World. Thereafter, Frenchmen continued to purchase beaver furs, but it became more consequence. It was his responsibility to find settlers and to cultivate the land, but the area belonged to him.

This was the first time La Salle had a free hand, and he used it to the utmost. Within a year of being granted the fief he had named it *La Chine* (China), to represent his hope that the fast-running water in the neighborhood would one day carry him all the way to the riches of China and Japan. La Salle was successful in attracting settlers and within a year he had made La Chine (today it is Lachine, a suburb of Montreal) into one of the more settled areas in the neighborhood. Had La Salle been content with this, he could have risen slowly but surely in the annals of New France, and his name, like that of men like Pierre

and more difficult for Canadian colonists to find the beaver, which had been trapped out along the St. Lawrence River. Thus began one of the great sagas of European colonization of America: the move inland for beaver skins.

Frenchmen followed the beaver to Lake Ontario, and later went all the way to Lake Superior. The Dutch remained in Manhattan and Albany (which they called New Amsterdam and Fort Orange) but they hired members of the Five Nations of Iroquois (more about them in the next chapter) to hunt and trap beaver far away. By the time La Salle arrived, in 1667, both New France and New York were expanding to the west to find new sources of beaver.

The beaver market began to suffer in the 1680s, and by 1700 most of the beaver along the Great Lakes had been trapped out. A decline in the number of furs trapped and sold began, but late in the eighteenth century the craze began once more. North Americans, by this time independent of Great Britain, led the way in trapping beaver as far west as the Rocky Mountains, leading to a second crash in the beaver market, around 1850.

Scientists lamented the near-extinction of the beaver, but the animal made a remarkable comeback in the twentieth century. A protected species in both Canada and the United States, the beaver is about as numerous today as it was before the arrival of Europeans in the seventeenth century.

Boucher (the founder of Boucherville) would be known to us today as that of a hard-working merchant of Montreal. But, as the Jesuit fathers had predicted, La Salle found it difficult to stick to a safe and narrow course.

The Western Country

West, to French-Canadians of La Salle's time, meant anything beyond Montreal, and it was this land that La Salle wished to see. Like many men of his time, he was dazzled by the idea of a northwest passage, one to carry ships from the North Atlantic to the North Pacific. No such strait existed, but La Salle was not the last to carry out searches for it.

La Salle found an opportunity to exercise his wanderlust in 1669, when he joined a party of explorers and missionaries, headed for the western Great Lakes. He sold his fief at La Chine to raise the money for this. Francis Parkman noted in his biography of La Salle:

> This was to be his life pattern: to sacrifice the sure thing for a chimera [fantasy], to mortgage his very being, as it were, for a chance at the big prize beyond the distant horizon —akin to what poker players call drawing to an inside straight.

One of the missionaries, François Dollier de Casson, had a great reputation as a fearless explorer and it would have boosted La Salle's reputation to be in his company. Yet, as the little group reached the neighborhood of Niagara Falls, La Salle struck off on his own, with two or three French-Canadians for company. What followed has remained unknown.

It is possible that La Salle and his fellows reached the upper banks of the Ohio River (*Ohio* is an abbreviation of the Native American name, which meant "beautiful river"). More likely he and his fellows heard about the Ohio from some Native Americans, and they supposed it might one day lead them

LA CACCIA DEI CASTORI

During the seventeenth century, beavers were found throughout North America as far south as central Mexico. Valued for their fur, trappers captured beavers and sold their pelts to Europe. After years of unlimited trapping by settlers and Native Americans, the beaver population, which was once more than 60 million, is currently estimated to be between 10 and 15 million.

to some sort of northwest passage. La Salle was still thinking of *western* exploration rather than southern.

Frenchmen before La Salle had heard of the Beautiful River, but sometime in the 1670s, it began appearing on French maps. Whether La Salle played any part in this is impossible to say.

La Salle disappears from the historical record between 1669 and 1672. In that time he continued to hold his fief at La Chine, and he doubtless did some exploring, but very few of his actions found their way into the public record. It was not until 1672, when a new governor appeared, that La Salle began to make frequent appearances in the chronicles of New France.

The Norman
and the Gascon

La Salle was an ideal Norman, meaning he was an adventurous type of person and aware of his ancestral roots. Descended from Viking warriors and Christian crusaders, he doubtlessly wished to carve a place in the history books for himself. Happily, he met, in the autumn of 1672, the new governor-general of Canada.

Louis de Buade, Count Frontenac

Louis de Buade, Count of Frontenac and Pallau, arrived in Quebec City in September 1672. Appointed governor-general of Canada, he came to this remote outpost as the representative of King Louis XIV.

Count Frontenac was as much a Gascon as La Salle was a Norman. If Normans were renowned for their ability in exploration and trade, then Gascons (*Gascony* meant most of southwestern France) were famous as storytellers, adventurers, and

As governor-general of New France (Quebec), Louis de Buade, the Count de Frontenac, supported a policy of colonial expansion. He established several forts in Native American territory on the Great Lakes and engaged in several battles with the Iroquois.

duelists: it is no coincidence that d'Artagnan, the most famous
of the Three Musketeers, hailed from southern France.

Born in Paris in 1622, Count Frontenac was a godson of
King Louis XIII. He had entered the military at an early age, and
by the time he came to Canada in 1672, he was both a brigadier-
general and a member of the king's court. Frontenac came from
a much more glorified background than La Salle, but the two
shared several things in common, most notably their dislike of
obeying orders. Just as La Salle had left the Jesuits, Frontenac
had quarreled with his military superiors on many occasions.
La Salle and Frontenac also shared an adventurous—one might
say, reckless—spirit. La Salle often disregarded a sure thing in
favor of a risky one; Count Frontenac had gambled away the
better part of two fortunes at the French court. La Salle came to
Canada in search of a new fortune; the same could be said for
the count.

Handsome Lake

In the spring of 1673, Count Frontenac set out from Montreal
with about 1,000 men, which represented a very high percent-
age of the total population (French Canada's population had,
by now, risen to about 7,000). His objective was to create a fort
and trading post on the banks of what the Native Americans
called Handsome Lake (today we call it Lake Ontario).

La Salle was in the entourage that ventured out from
Montreal. It is not certain when he first met Count Frontenac,
but it appears the two took to each other at once. If La Salle
was quieter and more introspective than most Normans, then
Count Frontenac was even friendlier and more outspoken than
most Gascons. In some cases, a friendship between two such
men would seem unlikely, but the governor and the fur trader
hit it off at once.

In early July, the French came to the head of Lake Ontario,
where its waters spill into the Saint Lawrence River. There, on

the north side of the Handsome Lake, Count Frontenac began building a stone fort, both to control the fur trade and to intimidate the Five Nations of Iroquois, who lived in what is now upstate New York.

A group of Iroquois chiefs came to the new fort to meet with Count Frontenac, who greeted them with these words:

> Children! . . . I am glad to see you here, where I have had a fire lighted for you to smoke by, and for me to talk to you. You have done well, my children, to obey the command of your Father. Take courage: you will hear his word, which

THE FIVE NATIONS

Sometime around 1570, a remarkable Native American leader, possessed of charismatic gifts and a new vision, presented his idea to the Iroquois: that they should live in eternal peace with each other. Deganawidah (some say he was a Huron, others say he was of the Onondaga tribe) explained his dream to Hiawatha, a Mohawk, and together they established the great Council Fire of Onondaga, where Syracuse, New York, now stands.

The Mohawk, Oneida, Onondaga, Cayuga, and Seneca all spoke the same language and shared many cultural similarities, but they were five separate nations before Deganawidah and Hiawatha, and so they remained. Under the leadership of these two men, the Five Nations of Iroquois pledged peace with one another but eternal vigilance against their common foes. By the time the French arrived in Canada, and by the time the Dutch came to Manhattan and Albany, the Five Nations were the greatest power brokers in the northeast part of today's United States.

No one knows exactly why, but the Five Nations became the most skillful and aggressive warriors of their time. Though other tribes, such as the Abenaki to the north or the Illinois to the west, might beat them in a battle, or even two in a row, the Five Nations nearly always won is full of peace and tenderness. For do not think that I have come for war. My mind is full of peace, and she walks by my side.

Whether the Iroquois chiefs believed Count Frontenac is difficult to say, but they were impressed by the 1,000 French, drawn up in military array, and by the rapid construction of the fort. For the moment, they, too, spoke of peace.

As the summer ended, Count Frontenac returned to Montreal and then Quebec. He and La Salle had become fast friends, and they both learned the good news that two Frenchmen had

their wars. In part this was because of their united front; in part, it was because of the wisdom of their chiefs. But most of all it was due to the ferocity with which they practiced the art of war.

Other tribes fought hard and well, but none could compete with the cunning and speed of the Iroquois. Warriors of the Five Nations traveled faster and fought harder than their opponents, and the unlucky man who fell into their clutches was usually subjected to severe torture. The Iroquois, like many Native Americans, often ate the hearts of enemies that they considered especially valiant, hoping that consuming the organ would give them the quality of their opponents.

The Five Nations became allies with the Dutch at Albany, and when Manhattan and Albany came under English rule they befriended them as well. The Five Nations held great hatred for the French in Canada, most likely because Samuel de Champlain—the founder of New France—had fought against them in 1609. His use of firearms won that battle, but it also earned Canada the everlasting enmity of the Iroquois.

In the early 1660s, the Five Nations had the French at their mercy, attacking settlers any time they left the safety of their houses and palisades. In 1665, two years before La Salle arrived, King Louis XVI sent the Carignan Regiment to Canada. These tough veterans defeated the Iroquois and made them sue for peace. In the first 10 years of La Salle's time in Canada, there was an uneasy peace between the French and the Five Nations.

found their way to yet another passageway, the greatest one yet found.

The Father of Waters

As described above, Count Frontenac arrived in Quebec in the autumn of 1672 and had his new fort built in the summer of 1673. In that same year, Father Jacques Marquette and Louis Joliet (also spelled Jolliet)—whose names are commemorated in many Midwestern places today—found their way to the Mississippi.

Born in France in 1637, Jacques Marquette entered the Jesuit order as a young man. He crossed the ocean in 1666 (just one year before La Salle), and, after some time in the area of Quebec City, went to the Great Lakes as a missionary. Born in Quebec in 1645, Louis Joliet was the son of a wagon maker. He, too, studied with the Jesuits, but he left the order in his late teens to become a merchant in the burgeoning fur trade.

In the winter of 1672, soon after he arrived in Canada, Count Frontenac commissioned Louis Joliet to explore in the Far West. Joliet set out that winter, and by spring of 1673 he was in the extreme western part of Lake Huron, where he linked up with Father Marquette. On May 17, 1673, the two leaders and five other Frenchmen set out on a quest, searching for the body of water the Native Americans called Mississippi, or Father of Waters.

The early part of their route paralleled the northern part of Lake Michigan, and they soon entered Green Bay, which was then labeled the Bay of Puans on most maps. Other Frenchmen had come this far before, but none had been as interested in mapping and charting the region. Marquette, Joliet, and their companions canoed down Green Bay, and then found Lake Osh-kosh, which eventually led them to the Fox River. In the area now called Portage, Wisconsin, they made a portage of about a mile and a half, taking them from the waters of the Fox to those of the Wisconsin. Now they were in truly uncharted territory.

Marquette, Joliet, and their companions floated down the Wisconsin River until on June 17, one month after leaving St. Ignace, they entered the much-broader flow of the Mississippi, right about where Prairie du Chien stands today. The Jesuit and the merchant immediately understood they had found one of the keys to navigation in the American West, for never, with the possible exception of the St. Lawrence, had they seen so strong a river.

Marquette and Joliet canoed almost 200 miles (321 km) along the great river without seeing any Native Americans, but late in June they met with a large group from the Illinois tribe, the people for whom both the river and the state are now named. Marquette described meeting the chief:

> When we reached the village of the great captain, we saw him in the entrance of his cabin, between two old men, all three erect and naked, and holding their calumet [decorated ceremonial pipe] turned toward the sun. He harangued us in a few words, congratulating us upon our arrival. He afterward offered us his calumet, and made us smoke while we entered his cabin, where we received all their kind attentions.

Marquette and Joliet were not the first Frenchmen to "smoke" the calumet; nor were they the last. The calumet refers both to the pipe of peace itself, and to the ceremony, which included singing, dancing, and smoking. The calumet ceremony established peace between those who performed it, and the presence of the pipe of peace meant that no blood could be shed. The Illinois chief gave a long oration, which praised the two leaders:

> I thank thee, Black Gown [Marquette], and thee O Frenchman [Joliet]…for having taken so much trouble to come and visit us. Never has the heart been so beautiful, or the sun so bright as today; never has our river been so calm or so free of rocks.

Marquette and Joliet were not the first Europeans to discover the Native American art of oratory, but their record of the expedition gives us a good glimpse into what the Illinois considered proper hospitality. Two decades later, a French artist depicted an Illinois chief holding the calumet aloft during

In 1673, Father Jacques Marquette and fur trader Louis Joliet were the first Europeans to come into contact with Native Americans east of Arkansas since Hernando de Soto's expedition in the 1540s. Their goal was to explore unsettled territory from the Great Lakes to the Gulf of Mexico for the colonial power of France. Along the way, Marquette and Joliet met with many Native Americans, including the Illinois (*above*).

a ceremony, and the image has become part of our modern-day visualization of the Mississippi River tribes.

Leaving the Illinois tribe, Marquette and Joliet paddled south. The current was at their back, and the seven Frenchmen made rapid progress, canoeing past the entrance of the Missouri River (they were the first Europeans to note its muddy quality) and that of the Ohio River. As they progressed, Marquette and Joliet became convinced that this, the Father of Waters, would eventually culminate in the southern sea rather than the western one. They were disappointed, for, like many Frenchmen of the time, they hoped for a northwest passage, a means of reaching the Pacific Ocean, but their contribution to the geography of their time was more important than their dashed hopes.

The further south they went, the more Marquette and Joliet worried about the possibility of meeting Spaniards. Although France and Spain were not at war—far from it—since the time of Hernando de Soto, the Spanish kings had decreed that the lands and waters de Soto explored were off limits to the subjects of any other monarch. As they neared the confluence of the Arkansas and Mississippi rivers, Marquette and Joliet saw iron tools and even weapons among some of the Native Americans, things that could only have come from trade with Spaniards.

Marquette and Joliet spent some days with the Arkansas tribe, in the area where the river of the same name flowed into the Mississippi, but then decided to turn back for Canada. Both men wished to carry their mission to its fullest extent; both wished to see where the Mississippi entered the Gulf of Mexico. But if something happened to them, neither the governor-general of Canada nor the King of France would ever learn of their discoveries. So, with some sadness, the two leaders turned the little party of seven back north. This time they had to battle the current.

The Chicago Portage

The Frenchmen made good time on their return trip, excellent time considering they had to paddle against the strength of the Mississippi. Speaking to different Native American groups, they learned of another, perhaps shorter, way to reach their starting point at St. Ignace. In August, the Frenchmen left the Father of Waters for the Illinois River, which took them very close to where the city of Chicago now stands (it was then a completely open and empty place). There was some hard carrying of the canoes, but Marquette and Joliet won distinction as the first Europeans to use the "Chicago Portage" between the Illinois and Chicago rivers. Soon afterward, they were on Lake Michigan, paddling for home.

The Forty-third Rapid

Marquette and Joliet arrived at St. Ignace in September 1673. They were welcomed as returning heroes, and indeed their mission of exploration had been very successful. For it to have its fullest effect, they needed to get word to the governor-general of Canada, but it was too late in the season for them to travel to Montreal. So, both men spent the winter on the Great Lakes, and in the spring of 1674 they parted company. Father Marquette stayed at St. Ignace, continuing his missionary work, while Louis Joliet went by canoe over the Great Lakes, carrying his maps and charts of the lands they had seen.

Joliet crossed Lake Huron and Lake Ontario, and made his way up what is now the St. Lawrence Seaway, between Montreal and the Great Lakes. About eight miles (12.8 km) shy of his destination, at a place of rapids called La Chine, Joliet's canoe overturned, resulting in the deaths of two of his canoe men, and the loss of all his precious written materials. Virtually everything he had brought back from the memorable voyage of exploration disappeared into the St. Lawrence River, never to be seen again.

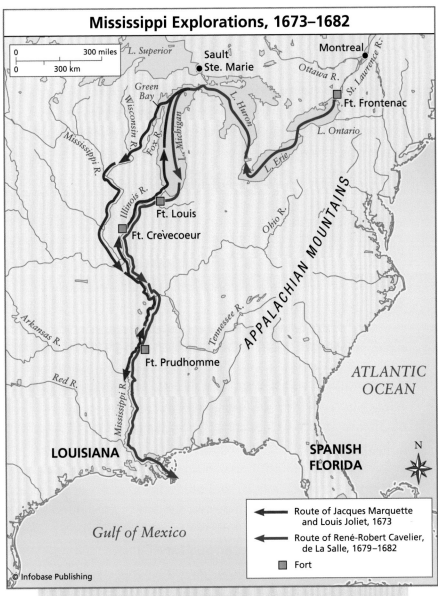

Mississippi Explorations, 1673–1682

0 — 300 miles
0 — 300 km

L. Superior

Sault Ste. Marie

Montreal

Ottawa R.

St. Lawrence R.

Green Bay

Ft. Frontenac

Wisconsin R.

Fox R.

L. Michigan

L. Huron

L. Ontario

Mississippi R.

L. Erie

Illinois R.

Ft. Louis

Ft. Crèvecoeur

Ohio R.

APPALACHIAN MOUNTAINS

Arkansas R.

Tennessee R.

Ft. Prudhomme

ATLANTIC OCEAN

Red R.

Mississippi R.

LOUISIANA

SPANISH FLORIDA

N

Gulf of Mexico

Route of Jacques Marquette and Louis Joliet, 1673
Route of René-Robert Cavelier, de La Salle, 1679–1682
Fort

© Infobase Publishing

Marquette and Joliet hoped to find an all-water route from the Great Lakes region to the Gulf of Mexico. The French wanted to begin to build forts along the Mississippi, place a barrier between themselves and the English colonies, and expand the Catholic faith. Although their journey was curtailed due to evidence that the Spanish were nearby, the information gained paved the way for the expedition of Robert de La Salle in 1679.

Heartbroken over the loss of the written materials, Joliet wrote to Count Frontenac:

> I had escaped every peril from the Indians. I had passed forty-two rapids, and was on the point of disembarking, full of joy at the success of so long and difficult an enterprise, when my canoe capsized, after all the danger seemed over.

Louis Joliet's career was not over. He would remake many of the maps from what was in his head, and in the years to come he would be one of the most noted pilots on the St. Lawrence River.

Father Marquette's career was nearly over. He succumbed to illness two years after his remarkable journey of discovery, dying in what is now Illinois.

One of the many ironies of seventeenth-century French exploration is that Louis Joliet's canoe capsized right by the settlement created by the man who would one day fulfill Joliet and Marquette's dream. They were the first Frenchmen to see and paddle on the Mississippi, but La Salle would be the first to travel the Father of Waters all the way to where the fresh water turned to salt.

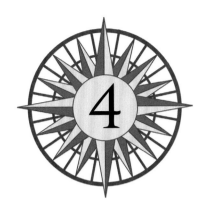

The Father
of Waters

Soon after learning of Father Marquette and Louis Joliet's voyage of discovery, La Salle sailed for France. He had been away for nearly seven years.

King and Court

In 1674, the king of France, Louis XIV, was nearing the peak of his power and influence. Born in 1638, Louis was five years older than La Salle. He had come to the throne in 1661, and had guided the country, ever since, in the direction of martial glory (the French call it *la gloire*).

When La Salle went to France in 1674, the center of the court was still in Paris; just a few years later, it would shift to the country estate of Versailles, about 12 miles (19 km) to the south. La Salle came, like so many other adventurers of his time, as a petitioner, asking King Louis for money, a title, and for assistance in future explorations. He soon found that it was not easy to see the "Sun King," as Louis was frequently called.

La Salle did have a strong recommendation from Count Frontenac, who wrote to Jean-Baptiste Colbert, minister of the marine and the colonies, that:

> [La Salle] is a man of intelligence and ability, more capable than anybody else I know here to accomplish every kind of enterprise and discovery which may be entrusted to him, as he has the most perfect knowledge of the state of the country, as you will see if you are disposed to give him a few moments of audience.

Minister Colbert was busy indeed, and La Salle found it necessary to bribe a functionary of the court just to obtain an audience. This bribe, of about 2,000 livres (the currency of France until 1795), would be followed by others over the years, and La Salle would eventually be led to financial ruin through the greed of this court official. There was no help for it, however, because the Sun King and his ministers were much more interested in European affairs than American ones. It took bribes such as this and recommendations such as Frontenac's for someone like La Salle to see the minister at all.

Minister Colbert, and King Louis as well, were pleased by what they heard of the state of affairs in Canada. La Salle told the minister about the fort at the head of Lake Ontario, explaining that it would allow French-Canadian merchants to win the fur trade of the Upper Great Lakes. Minister Colbert was impressed enough to recommend to the king that La Salle's request for a minor patent of nobility be granted, and in 1675, the king gave his assent to the document that declared:

> We have ennobled, and by these patents, signed by Our hand, do ennoble and decorate with the title and quality of Nobility, the said Cavelier, together with his wife and children, posterity and issue, both male and female, born and to be born in lawful wedlock.

In 1675, La Salle returned to France to petition King Louis XIV for permission to explore the Mississippi (*depicted above*). Not only did the king give La Salle his consent, he rewarded the explorer with a patent of nobility.

Doubtless this was very gratifying to La Salle, but the minor patent did not elevate him to the ranks of the nobles of the sword of Old France. Such men, like Count Frontenac, could trace the lines of their ancestors for centuries, and could point to royal favor over many generations. La Salle had made a beginning toward that end, but he still had a long way to go.

Louis XIV also confirmed La Salle in what had, until then, been a temporary position as governor of the fort on Lake Ontario. Whether it was out of gratitude toward his patron or sheer circumstance, La Salle named it Fort Frontenac.

Building

Returning to Canada in the summer of 1675, La Salle went passionately to work. He moved his permanent home to Fort Frontenac, and within a year he had changed the stone fort into a true, European-style fortification, complete with a trading post. His first fief, at La Chine, had been good enough in 1667, but to be commander of a fort that was potentially the most important post on the Great Lakes signified a major step forward. La Salle had the confidence and friendship of Count Frontenac, and he stood to make a fortune in the fur trade. At the same time that he reached a new height, La Salle also won the enemies that would dog him for the rest of his life.

When he first arrived in Canada, La Salle had made friends among the merchants of Montreal, men who had been in Canada a long time and who stood to profit from the increase in the fur trade. Yet once he became commandant of Fort Frontenac, La Salle became their enemy, for he intended to monopolize the profits from the furs coming in from Lake Ontario. The Montreal merchants had already moved to expand their business in other directions (some of them went as far north as Hudson's Bay), but La Salle's new position still made him a threat to their financial well-being. Sadly, La Salle's brother Jean agreed with them.

A New Design

Sometime in 1676, La Salle developed his most ambitious plan to date. He remembered, from his travels in 1669, the tales of the Ohio, or Beautiful River. To these he added the

SIBLING RIVALRY

It is almost impossible to say what went wrong in their relationship, but the historical record makes it plain that Jean Cavelier, the elder brother, and La Salle, the younger, were often at odds.

The elder by two years, Jean was a Sulpician priest and stayed religious all his life. La Salle had become a Jesuit but did not remain in the order. Jean came to Canada first, and when La Salle followed, the elder brother helped the younger to obtain the fief of La Chine, which he held through the good graces of the Sulpician Order. That was the last "brotherly" act of Jean Cavelier.

Between 1675 and 1678, La Salle fell deeply in debt, both to the merchants of Montreal and to a cousin in Old France. Because La Salle was exploring in the wilderness, Jean was his financial executor, acting on his behalf. Jean, who had by now become an abbot (head of a monastery), betrayed his younger brother, confiscating much of his property to pay debts, many of which were to Jean himself. Jean lined his pockets at his brother's expense and did not pay off the most pressing debts. The result was that La Salle was financially ruined, due partly by his brother's actions.

Normally, this would end the relationship, but La Salle remained cordial to his older brother. In 1684, when Jean asked to be included in La Salle's greatest enterprise, the younger brother agreed. Perhaps he had decided nothing worse could happen. Then again, he may have decided it was safer to have Jean along than to have him manage financial affairs in his absence.

stories told by Father Marquette and Louis Joliet of the Father of Waters. It was not a great leap to suppose that the former fed into the latter, but La Salle was one of the first to propose that France reach out and seize control of both of the rivers.

La Salle had no opportunity to speak with Father Marquette, who died in present-day Wisconsin in 1675, but he did meet with Louis Joliet. Count Frontenac, who had become enthused over Marquette and Joliet's discovery, also spoke to La Salle about the opportunities that existed in the West, and, in 1677, La Salle sailed for France for a second time. On this occasion, he brought a long memorial, which he presented to Minister Colbert:

> [The Western country] is nearly all so beautiful and fertile; so free from forests, and so full of meadows, brooks, and rivers; so abounding in fish, game, and venison, that one can find there in plenty, and with little trouble, all that is needful for the support of flourishing colonies.

La Salle made a pointed contrast to Canada, which, as he declared, suffered from a long winter and a hard, stony soil.

For a second time, La Salle had to pay a greedy court functionary, and this time the price was much higher. Between 1677 and 1678, this official extorted about 10,000 livres from La Salle, in order to allow him to present his memorial to the minister of the colonies. Yet it all seemed worthwhile when Louis XIV granted La Salle an exclusive patent for western exploration:

> We have permitted, and do hereby permit you, by these presents, signed by Our hand, to endeavor to discover the western part of New France, and for the execution of this enterprise, to construct forts wherever you deem necessary; which it is Our will that you shall hold on the same terms and conditions as Fort Frontenac. . . .We give you

full powers: on condition, however, that you shall finish this enterprise within five years, in default of which these patents shall be void and of none effect.

To us today, with our knowledge of American geography, five years seems plenty of time, but to La Salle, who was attempting to fill in the gaps of that geography, five years was short indeed. He naturally accepted the king's patent and prepared to leave for America. Not long before leaving, La Salle made the acquaintance of the man who would help him more than any other, Henry de Tonty.

Iron Hand

Tonty was born in Italy, sometime in 1650, but his parents moved north to France to settle in Paris soon after his birth. They had been leaders in a popular revolt against the government of Naples, and it was safer to be out of the country in the aftermath of its failure.

Tonty grew up in Paris, where his father became a banker, as well as a financial advisor to the government of Louis XIV. Tonty's father embezzled money by designing a life insurance plan so devious and complex that insurance executives still call it "Tontine." For this, he spent a number of years in the Bastille, the government prison near the center of Paris.

Henry de Tonty appears to have inherited none of his father's greed; adventure and glory, rather than money, won his interest. Tonty entered the French army at the age of 18, and served Louis XIV in a number of Mediterranean campaigns. While fighting in Sicily—not far from his Neapolitan birthplace—Tonty lost his right hand to an enemy grenade and was subsequently captured. As there was no doctor present, Tonty tended to the stump himself, and later he fashioned a metal replacement. Whether it was of iron, copper, or brass remains in dispute, but there is no doubt that he fitted the new implement, covered it with a glove, and that friends and foes alike called him "Iron Hand."

Tonty was in Paris, on army leave, when La Salle appeared in 1677. The two met through the graces of Louis, the Prince of Conti, who recommended Tonty to La Salle, suggesting that a man of such fortitude would make a good lieutenant for his explorations in America. La Salle and Tonty took to each other at once, and, over the next few years they became a formidable one-two combination, one as significant as that of Meriwether Lewis and William Clark or even of Robert E. Lee and Stonewall Jackson.

La Salle and Tonty left for Canada with high hopes. The plan was for them to build one ship on Lake Erie, which would carry furs, supplies, and men to the western side of the Great Lakes. Then another ship would be built on one of the major rivers flowing to the Mississippi. La Salle had a grand ambition, to master the navigation of the Great Lakes and the Illinois-Mississippi river basins.

The Great Falls

The first written description of Niagara Falls comes to us from the pen of Father Louis Hennepin, a Franciscan friar who became friendly with both La Salle and Tonty. Born in Belgium, Father Hennepin came to America around 1675. In the winter of 1678, he went to the Niagara region to assist in the building of the first ocean-going ship upon the Great Lakes:

> I went overland to view the great fall, the like whereof is not in the whole world. It is compounded of two great cross streams of water and two falls, with an isle sloping along the middle of it. The waters which fall from this vast height do foam and boil after the most hideous manner imaginable, making an outrageous noise, more terrible

Two of America's great waterfalls were brought to the world's attention after Father Louis Hennepin accompanied La Salle on voyages to explore the western part of New Canada. Hennepin made sketches and wrote about the great Niagara Falls (*above*) and the Saint Anthony Falls in present-day Minneapolis, the only waterfall on the Mississippi River.

than that of thunder; so that when the wind blows from the south their dismal roaring may be heard above fifteen leagues off.

Although Father Hennepin's measurement of the falls at about 600 feet (182 m) high was an exaggeration, it became the standard one for the next 50 years. Thousands of Europeans received their first description in words from his pen and their first view of the falls from a drawing that accompanied his first book, published in 1683.

Father Hennepin had time to write, but he also sawed planks and drove nails along with the rest of the company La Salle brought to the Niagara region. They set up camp in the area just south of the falls and commenced building a 40-ton (36,287-kilograms) ship, which La Salle called the *Griffin* (*Le Griffon*). La Salle had to hasten back to Fort Frontenac to deal with his creditors, and Father Hennepin and Henry de Tonty oversaw the building of the ship, which was ready by the summer of 1679.

Griffins and Crows

The ship's name came from the mythical beast that decorated the family arms of Count Frontenac. This was another way of honoring his patron, and La Salle also said he would make the *Griffin* (Count Frontenac) fly above the crows, by which he meant the black-robed Jesuits (Count Frontenac disliked the Jesuits as heartily as did La Salle).

The ship was launched in the area of what is now Buffalo, New York, in early August of 1679 (see map on page 31). This was one of La Salle's signal accomplishments. Every previous trip across Lake Erie—whether done by Native Americans or Frenchmen—had been by birch bark canoe, hugging the waterline. Now, for the first time, a ship that lifted high above the waves could travel over the area the Native Americans called Karegnondi.

Michilimackinac

La Salle, Tonty, and Father Hennepin sailed west, across Lake Erie. A few days of calm sailing brought them to the western end of Lake Erie and into the narrow body of water that parallels modern-day Detroit. The *Griffin* sailed past Detroit and out onto Lake Saint Clair, which brought them to Lake Huron. Theirs was the first ocean-going ship to make this voyage.

Father Hennepin described a frightening moment as the *Griffin* crossed Lake Huron:

> The 26th [of August] we had so violent a storm that we brought down our yards and topmasts and let the ship drive at the mercy of the wind, knowing no place to run into shelter ourselves. Monsieur de La Salle, notwithstanding he was a courageous man, began to fear, and told us we were undone; whereupon everybody fell on his knees to say his prayers and prepare himself for death.

This was the first, but by no means the last, time that Father Hennepin wrote disapprovingly of La Salle. It is unclear whether Hennepin was envious of La Salle's reputation or if he wished to make one for himself, but there were many occasions of his talking down the expedition's leader.

The wind abated the next day, and the *Griffin*, a little the worse for wear, sailed into the trading post at Michilimackinac.

Founded by Jesuit priests and fur traders, Michilimackinac was on present-day Mackinac Island, very close to the confluence between Lakes Huron and Michigan. Michilimackinac had a population of several hundred Native Americans, priests, and fur traders, making it the most populous place on the Great Lakes. La Salle made a great impression by sailing the *Griffin* in, but this was also the home of many of his enemies. The Jesuits knew him as one who had left their order, and the fur merchants were connected with those of Montreal.

Happily, there were many furs in the area. La Salle had planned ahead, sending merchants and trappers, and there were a great many beaver skins to load aboard the *Griffin*. It was not enough to solve all of his financial difficulties, but La Salle looked forward to making some real inroads on the loans he had rung up over the past two years.

A month after arriving at Michilimackinac, La Salle and the entire party sailed into Lake Michigan and progressed to

Green Bay, by the same route that Marquette and Joliet had employed in 1673. Once in Green Bay, La Salle ordered the captain of the *Griffin* to return to Michilimackinac, to take on some extra materials, and then to sail all the way back to the Niagara Falls area, to unload and sell the accumulated furs.

Fort Miami

La Salle and Tonty also split up for a number of weeks. La Salle and a group of Frenchmen canoed to the southeastern side of Lake Michigan, where they began to build Fort Miami, right about where St. Joseph, Michigan, stands today. Tonty and another group explored the Green Bay region, then rejoined La Salle at the new fort.

Having heard nothing from his ship's crew, it was about this time that La Salle became anxious over the *Griffin*. Unbeknownst to La Salle, the *Griffin* had been lost in a storm on Lake Michigan.

La Salle, Tonty, and about 30 others—including Father Hennepin and two other Franciscan friars—left Fort Miami early in December 1679. Learning from the local Native Americans of a portage that would take them to the Father of Waters, the Frenchmen went south to what is now South Bend, Indiana (the home of Notre Dame University), and found the five-mile (eight-km) portage between the St. Joseph and Kankakee rivers. This was a milestone in La Salle's explorations, for, as one historian put it:

> Until his arrival at this point we might consider his journey all an upstream process. He came up the St. Lawrence, up the Niagara, up the Detroit, and up the St. Joseph. Even crossing the [Great] Lakes seemed upstream. After portaging over this strip of less than five miles, the rest of the journey was downstream—down the Kankakee, down the Illinois, down the Mississippi to the Gulf.

SHIPS AND STORMS ON THE LAKES

Even a casual glance at Lakes Ontario, Erie, Huron, Michigan, and Superior reveals that these are no ordinary bodies of fresh water. Though they are surrounded by land, these lakes are closer to inland oceans than we might think.

Those who study the Great Lakes and their history believe that there are some autumn and winter storms there which equal or even exceed the violence of ocean ones. This is because the Lakes are in a zone where climates meet: warm air coming from the Gulf of Mexico clashes with cold air coming down from Canada. It comes as no surprise, therefore, to learn that the Lakes have seen some true "whopper" storms over the course of time.

The storm that claimed the *Griffin*, in 1679, was only an average one, but, as shipping on the Lakes grew, so did the number of losses and fatalities. By about 1890, the Lakes had more commercial ships and pleasure boats than any other place in the world, ranging from big ships that carried coal and iron across Lake Superior, to fancy yachts that took wealthy passengers from Detroit to Chicago. All those boat trips, and all the storms of the autumn season, led to many losses on the Great Lakes.

The best known of all shipping losses on the Lakes is the *Edmund Fitzgerald*, which went down in a major November storm in 1975. The loss was commemorated in song.

Days after reaching the Illinois River—which was much broader than the Kankakee—La Salle and his companions found a large but empty Native American town, right above where Starved Rock State Park (the name "Starved Rock" came later) stands. La Salle took some Indian corn from this deserted spot and pushed south-by-southwest, along the Illinois River, until reaching where Peoria, Illinois, stands today. He met several thousand Illinois tribal people. The first meeting was tense, but La Salle won the Illinois over with a mixture of condescension and fearlessness. It must be said that he was a master of diplomacy, never demonstrating fear, but always showing himself ready to make friends when possible.

To the Illinois, La Salle revealed his plan to build a ship there, on the banks of their river. This ship, he told them, would sail down the Illinois to the Mississippi, then all the way to the Gulf of Mexico. The Illinois seemed both perplexed and displeased by this. They told him of enormous beasts (crocodiles, perhaps) that would devour him and his men, but La Salle was undaunted. He would go to where the Father of Waters ran into salt water.

La Salle, Tonty, Hennepin, and the rest began building a ship just outside the town at Peoria, but six of the Frenchmen deserted soon after their conversation with the Illinois Indians: the idea of crocodiles and other terrors, persuaded them to flee. La Salle continued to build both the beginnings of a ship and the beginnings of a fort, which he named Fort Crevecoeur (Fort Heartbreak) because of the desertion of his men.

Most early historians of La Salle blamed the men for their cowardice, but later ones point out that La Salle's men were seldom paid. La Salle was virtually bankrupt; he did not know what had happened to the *Griffin*; and there was every likelihood that his men would never receive any pay. Small wonder that they deserted him and his enterprise.

On March 1, 1680, the remaining Frenchmen split into three groups. La Salle and two others started the long trek back to Niagara, where he would learn what had happened to the *Griffin*. Father Hennepin and two others went west, looking for other possible routes to the Mississippi River. Tonty and the balance of the party continued to work on the ship, which they hoped would be ready upon La Salle's return.

The Iroquois War

While La Salle returned to Niagara (to learn the *Griffin* was lost), Tonty kept his men hard at work building their new ship. Many of these men, however, soon deserted. If any further proof of Tonty's loyalty and strength were required, it was supplied by his conduct during the war that followed.

In the summer of 1680, about 1,000 Iroquois warriors came west toward the Illinois country. They were jealous of the fur trade, and believed that La Salle and the Illinois tribe might one day take it away from them. Luckily, Tonty learned of the Iroquois invasion just in time.

The Iroquois

The Five Nations of Iroquois had been suspiciously quiet during the past two years. Even La Salle's building of the *Griffin* in the country of the Seneca (part of the Iroquois) had not prompted any outburst or attacks on the French settlements. Still, the Five Nations bided their time, and in the spring of 1680 they came west with about 600 warriors, armed to the teeth.

Tonty was with the Illinois at the time, and he and they were equally alarmed to hear of the Iroquois advance. There were about 600 Illinois warriors in the area, but very few of them had muskets, and few were renowned fighters like the Iroquois. Determined to put a good face on the situation, Tonty went out to meet the enemy just as the battle was about to begin:

> When I was within gunshot the Iroquois shot at us, seized me, took the necklace [of wampum] from my hand, and one of them plunged a knife into my breast, wounding a rib near the heart. However, having recognized me, they carried me into the midst of the camp, and asked me what I came for.

Gasping for breath because of the knife wound, Tonty told them he was astonished to find them in the Illinois Country, that the Illinois were under the protection of the governor of Canada, and that he would defend them to the last. He also made it seem that there were 100 armed Frenchmen in his camp, although there were actually fewer than a dozen.

> On this they were greatly irritated against me, and held a council on what they should do with me. There was a man behind me with a knife in his hand, who every now and then lifted up my hair.

Whether it was out of respect for Tonty's bravery, or out of fear of what the governor of Canada might do, the Iroquois spared his life. Tonty was returned to the camp of the Illinois. They must be brave, he said, or the Iroquois would spot their fear and act accordingly.

Days passed, with skirmishes rather than a set-piece battle. The Iroquois eventually learned that Tonty had deceived them as to the number of Frenchmen in his camp. They summoned him to another council, where they handed him a set of wampum and a series of messages (handing a wampum bead with each message was a tribal practice):

> The first two packets were to inform Monsieur de Frontenac that they would not eat his children, and that he should not be angry at what they had done; the third, a plaster for my wound; the fourth, some oil to rub on my own and Father Zenoble's limbs, on account of the long journey we had taken; the fifth, that the sun was bright; the sixth, that we should profit by it and depart the next day for the French settlements.

Tonty had done all that he could. On the morning of the next day, he, Father Zenoble, and the other few Frenchmen left the Illinois camp, headed for Fort Miami.

Ruin

La Salle, on arriving at Niagara, found ruin staring him straight in the face. He learned that the *Griffin* was lost and that none of her cargo of beaver furs had ever reached Niagara, much less the pockets of his many creditors. Making things even worse, La Salle received a message from Tonty telling him of the betrayal of most of the men working on the new ship.

If ever there was a time for a man to quit, La Salle had reached that point. Since 1678, when he received Louis XIV's commission, La Salle had had two ships wrecked (one in the St. Lawrence River, the other on the Great Lakes), and had witnessed the treachery of many of his men and the shameless aggression of his creditors. Nonetheless, La Salle did not budge from his desire, which was to open a new fur-trading empire in the Far West. One can certainly claim that he had no choice; by now, he was in so deep that he could only go forward.

Rather than despair, La Salle gathered a new, more loyal, body of men, and lay in wait for the traitors, whom Tonty had told him were coming his way. La Salle surprised them on Lake Ontario, killed two, and accepted the rest back into his company.

An Alliance with the Tribes of the Lower Great Lakes

Leaving the Niagara region, La Salle hastened back to the Illinois Country, where he found the ruins of Fort Crevecouer. He saw the scrawled message, "We are all savages," but had no way of knowing what had happened to Tonty and the others. La Salle continued down the Illinois River, looking for signs of Tonty. Failing to find either his lieutenant or his bones, La Salle returned to Fort Miami, at the southeast end of Lake Michigan, to spend the winter (Tonty and the others rejoined him in the spring of 1681).

In the 1640s, the Iroquois began a series of wars against the Great Lakes tribes. In order to control the fur trade, they completely wiped out some tribes, like the Erie, and scattered others from their homelands. In response, La Salle established a trading agreement with the numerous tribes that had been warring with the Iroquois. Above, La Salle and his men enjoy a feast with the Illinois tribe.

La Salle turned his attention to building a great alliance with the tribes of the Great Lakes region. So long as the Five Nations of Iroquois were free to come west, they could wreck all his plans. So, in May 1681, La Salle held a great conference of tribes under an oak tree in what is now South Bend, Indiana (the council oak stood for centuries, finally falling to a storm in 1991).

After distributing presents (a necessity when holding a council), La Salle addressed the different tribes:

> He who is my master, and the master of all this country, is a mighty chief, feared by the whole world; but he loves peace, and the words of his lips are for good alone. He is called the King of France, and he is the mightiest among the chiefs beyond the great water. His goodness reaches even to your dead, and his subjects come among you to raise them up to life.

La Salle's reference to death and the life beyond probably made little impact, for the Native Americans were used to forming their own religious beliefs. But his words about the power of Louis XIV may have had some effect. He continued:

> You ought, then, to live at peace with your neighbors, and above all with the Illinois. You have had causes of quarrel with them; but their defeat [at the hands of the Iroquois] has avenged you. Be content with the glory of having obliged them to ask for it. You have an interest in preserving them; since, if the Iroquois destroy them, they will next destroy you. Let us all obey the Great King, and live together in peace, under his protection.

Whether it was La Salle's words or the presents he distributed, no one can say, but the Native Americans who came to the Council Oak seem to have heeded his message. For the next several years, the tribes of the Lower Great Lakes banded together to resist the Five Nations of Iroquois.

With this conference, La Salle accomplished one of his greatest successes. No previous Frenchmen had been able to bring about peace between the different Great Lakes tribes. So long as they remained united against the Iroquois, La Salle could continue his plan to follow the Father of Waters to its ultimate destination.

5

To the Gulf

LA SALLE AND TONTY FINALLY REUNITED IN THE SUMMER OF 1681. Both men could hardly believe the tales of the other, for they had each gone through incredible hardships. Yet they had come through.

Money Lenders

La Salle had one more piece of financial business to conclude. Even now, with peace established among the Great Lakes tribes, he had to return to Montreal one more time, in an attempt to satisfy his creditors. They were pressing on him more than ever, to the extent that he was a ruined man. Even his cousin, Francis Plet, had no qualms about charging him 40 percent interest on a loan. In an effort to at least win some breathing room, La Salle signed a will that allotted virtually everything he possessed (at Fort Frontenac) and everything he might earn in the future to his creditors. It was a sad moment.

As one of La Salle's biographers has written:

> It portended the explorer's loss of all potential monetary benefit from his enterprises. His future successes, however grand, were pledged to pay for his past failures. Even a post controlling the mouth of the Mississippi would have been but the means of satisfying his creditors, who held him firmly in their grip.

Chicago

Father Marquette and Louis Joliet, in 1673, had been the first Frenchmen to use the Chicago portage, between Lake Michigan and the Des Plaines River, right where the modern city of Chicago now stands. Up until 1681, La Salle had always used the St. Joseph-Kankakee River portage, as his way of reaching the Illinois. But in the winter of 1681–1682, he decided on a different path.

Tonty and about six other Frenchmen went first, crossing Lake Michigan in the dead of winter. They found the Chicago portage open but the Des Plaines River completely iced over. They began the difficult task of transporting everything by sledges. Axe, shovel, pick, and saw—all were used as the Frenchmen cleared the way for La Salle, who, with the main body of French and Native Americans, arrived on January 6, 1682.

La Salle had chosen 27 hardy Frenchmen and a slightly smaller number of Native Americans, most of them Mohican or Abenaki. Ten of the Native Americans insisted on bringing women along, so the party added up to 54 persons, including La Salle, Tonty, and Father Membre, who left a stirring account of the journey. Together, they set off in early January, sledging across the portage and then the frozen river.

The exploring party made its way down the Illinois River, past abandoned Fort Crevecoeur, and then picked up speed as the current added strength to their paddle work. By the sixth of February, they entered the Mississippi.

Cahokia is the site of an ancient Native American city near Collinsville, Illinois. The 2,200-acre (8.9 square kilometers) site contains about 109 man-made earthen mounds, including Monk's Mound (*above*), the largest pre-Columbian earthwork north of central Mexico. The Mississippian Indians had developed advanced societies centuries before the arrival of the first French explorers in the 1600s.

Marquette and Joliet, and perhaps a handful of other un-named Frenchmen, had been here, but it was the first time for La Salle, Tonty, and most of their company. Here was a great river, big enough and swift enough that they called it Le Fleuve, a distinction given only to one other American river, the St. Lawrence. La Salle named it Le Fleuve Colbert, in honor of the minister of the marine and the colonies.

Heading south, they soon reached the confluence of the Mississippi and Missouri rivers. La Salle did not give the

Missouri the name of "Big Muddy;" that designation came later; but he and his party were among the first to see just how much sediment the Missouri discharged into the Mississippi. Just a few miles below that confluence, they passed the area known as "Cahokia." They did not know that it had once been a site of great ceremonial significance to the Native Americans of the heartland, or that it contained an earthen mound as large as most of the Egyptian pyramids. That discovery had to wait until the early nineteenth century.

La Salle and Tonty knew enough about the Marquette and Joliet expedition to be able to predict some of what came next, but, even so, they were surprised by the strength and size of the Ohio River, which flowed in to their left, or east. Father Membre claimed that for about a hundred miles (160.9 km) below the Ohio, one could not stop because the banks of the Mississippi were so high and there was so much brush of varying types. It is difficult to verify his claim, for that area of the Mississippi River is well populated today, leading to a reduction in the wildlife and fauna. Moreover, the Mississippi changes its course, ever so slightly, over time, and the banks he saw in 1682 may not be the same that we see today.

Meeting the Native Americans

La Salle's party met few Native Americans in the first half of its journey, but as soon as they passed the Ohio River, the Frenchmen met numerous Native American tribes. Many of them were descendants of those who had met Hernando de Soto's Spaniards a century and a half earlier, and there were some alarms, but La Salle's skillful diplomacy usually kept problems to a minimum. One of the first big meetings was with the Arkansas tribe, which had been the last stopping point for Marquette and Joliet nine years before.

One Arkansas group seemed to pose a threat, so La Salle had his whole company paddle to the east bank of the river,

HENNEPIN'S ADVENTURES

Those who read the three books written by Father Hennepin have never been able to decide whether he was a monstrous liar, a daring and courageous man, or a little of both. Most scholars believe that the first book, published in 1683, is fairly accurate, and that he went to literary extremes in the next two, published in 1697 and 1701, respectively.

It is certain that Father Hennepin, along with two other Frenchmen, set out from Fort Creveceour in the spring of 1680. La Salle commissioned them to explore the upper reaches of the Illinois River. Hennepin was not the leader of the little party, although in his writings he makes it sound as if he were.

The three men were captured by Sioux warriors in July. Other Frenchmen had, perhaps, met small groups of Sioux before, but Hennepin's description of these warriors—which rings true to the modern ear—is the first detailed description of that warlike group of tribes. The Sioux he met in 1680 were not the hard-riding horsemen of the Great Plains, but their more sedentary cousins of the eastern woodlands. Even

where he put it in a state of readiness for war. Seeing his preparations, the Arkansas became friendlier, and soon there was an exchange of gifts and performance of ceremonies. La Salle noted that the group had a variety of copper and iron instruments, which, he surmised, could only have come from trade with Spaniards somewhere in the Gulf of Mexico. He was as close as Marquette and Joliet, and closer than he had ever been to the fulfillment of his dream.

The Sun King

All Frenchmen knew that Louis XIV had long ago claimed the sun as his personal emblem. The sun and its rays were depicted on tapestries, books, and even carved onto the barrels of French so, some of their descendants were among those who later fought the U.S. cavalry on the plains.

Hennepin went to all sorts of extreme measures to persuade the Sioux not to knock him and his fellows on the head. He may have succeeded in getting them to think he was a magician of the black arts. For whatever reason, the Sioux allowed them to live, and three months after they fell into captivity, Hennepin and the others were rescued by a French fur trader and explorer, Daniel Greysolon, Sieur du Luth, for whom the city of Duluth, Minnesota, is named.

Hennepin returned to France by 1683 and commenced writing. His first publication aroused only moderate attention, but his second and third stimulated great interest in North America. By then, he had forsaken loyalty to Louis XIV and France and pledged it to King William of England, to whom he dedicated his second book.

Hennepin gives himself too much credit in his books, but some of the adventures could not have been made up. They reflected North American life at that time. Though he can be accused of self-importance and vanity, Hennepin must also be conceded great courage. Very few Belgian friars ventured to America at that time, and almost no one—other than La Salle or Tonty—saw as much of the great new land as he did.

muskets and cannon. As they descended the lower part of the Mississippi, La Salle and his men encountered a group, the Natchez, who also claimed a special relationship with the sun.

La Salle was ill so Tonty went to meet the leader of the Natchez. Tonty described the meeting:

> When I was in his cabin he told me with a smiling countenance the pleasure he felt at the arrival of the French. I saw that one of his wives wore a pearl necklace. I presented her with ten yards of blue glass beads in exchange for it. She made some difficulty but the chief having told her to let me have it, she did so. I carried it to Monsieur de La Salle, giving him an account of all that I had seen, and told him that the chief intended to visit him the next day.

The Natchez chief—or king—came carried by his subjects, with men using something like brooms to sweep away all dust from his path. Truly, the Natchez leader lived sumptuously, as the embodiment of the sun. The Natchez remembered this day for generations to come, as it was the beginning of their relationship with the French.

River's End

By late March, La Salle, Tonty, and their companions saw signs that pointed to the imminent arrival of the sea. Sometimes they could smell salt in the distance. They witnessed the passing of birds overhead, the type that indicated to them that the ocean was near.

The Frenchmen were tired and hungry, a condition that nearly led to their demise. At one point, in the area of what is now New Orleans, they spotted what they thought was a village. They found a ruined place with carcasses of Native Americans and beasts. So hungry were they that the Frenchmen ate some of what they found before determining it was human flesh.

Nauseated, weary, and desiring an end to their journey, the French and Native Americans continued. On April 6, 1682, they found the Father of Waters divided into three separate channels. Sensing that the end was near, La Salle divided his men into three groups. Tonty took the middle channel, La Salle took the left, and another Frenchman took the right. Father Membre wrote that his group found the water turned to salt just 2 miles (3.2 km) after the split into three groups.

They reunited, and on April 9, 1682, La Salle had a large wooden cross erected and the armaments of Louis XIV placed on a post. Then he called out the immortal words that claimed the land, the waters, and the peoples for France. He named the mouth of the Mississippi River *La Louisiane*:

> In the name of the most high, mighty, invincible and victorious Prince, Louis the Great, by the Grace of God King of

After traveling down the Illinois River, La Salle finally made it to the Gulf of Mexico. On April 9, 1682, La Salle buried an engraved plate and a cross at the mouth of the Mississippi and claimed the territory for France. He called this territory Louisiana, after King Louis.

France and of Navarre, Fourteenth of that name, this ninth
day of April, one thousand six hundred and eighty-two,
I…do now take, in the name of his Majesty…possession
of this country of Louisiana, the seas, harbors, ports, bays,
adjacent straits, and all the nations, people, provinces, cit-
ies, towns, villages, mines, minerals, fisheries, streams and
rivers comprised in the extent of said Louisiana.

According to the European custom, La Salle had taken
possession and the area now belonged to France. Of course,
the Spaniards had an earlier claim based on the explorations
of Hernando de Soto, and the Native Americans—Natchez,
Quinipassa, Arkansas, and others—had a much better one.
But according to La Salle, the entire area now belonged to his
home country.

The Return

Had he more time, La Salle would have explored the region more
thoroughly but he and his men were entirely out of food. Like
Marquette and Joliet before, they feared they might not reach
home in order to tell of their exploits. Therefore, after leaving signs and marks of their presence, the French and Native
Americans headed for the Illinois Country, and then Canada.

It was not an easy trip.

First, the French came to battle with the Quinipassa.
This tribe was the most warlike of those near the Mississippi's
mouth, and its warriors nearly caught the French by surprise.
Only a last-minute alert saved La Salle and his men, who killed
two of the enemy, and then pushed on.

Wherever they stopped, the French sought Indian corn,
about the only food available at that time of the year. They
found enough to keep going, but the limited, unbalanced diet
made many of the men sick. La Salle himself fell ill as the
expedition came into the land of the Arkansas Indians. La
Salle had a strong constitution, which had saved him many

times, but he was at the end of his strength. The worries and concerns—financial as well as physical—had taxed him to his limit. Realizing this, La Salle ordered Tonty to take the main body of men north, all the way to Michilimackinac, while he remained in the land of the Arkansas, hopefully to recover.

No-man's-land

La Salle was ill for almost 60 days, during which he was tended by Father Membre. His illness may have been a bad fever, but it is also possible he had suffered a minor stroke, brought on by the fatigues of the journey and the excesses of his lifestyle of the past few years. In either case, he recovered slowly and was only able to ascend the Mississippi toward the end of the summer. When he returned to Fort Miami, and then to Michilimackinac, La Salle may have felt that the world was pulled out from under him. Here he was, returning with the biggest news of exploration heard since the time of Samuel de Champlain, yet he could not get credit or reward for his accomplishment. Not only were his creditors united against him, but he had lost his strongest protector, Governor Frontenac.

Count Frontenac had been a contentious governor from the beginning, and Louis XIV and Colbert, the minister of the colonies, had heard many reports of his irrational and erratic behavior. Louis XIV finally issued the order for Frontenac's recall in the spring of 1682, with the news reaching Quebec that autumn. The king sent Joseph-Antoine de la Barre, a naval officer of many years experience, as Frontenac's replacement.

Frontenac had always been La Salle's strongest ally. With his removal, the explorer was in trouble. La Barre, the new governor, was predisposed to favor the merchants of Montreal and their belief that further exploration in the Far West was useless. La Barre came armed with instructions to dispossess La Salle of Fort Frontenac, on Lake Ontario, and Fort Saint Louis, in the Illinois Country.

All of this La Salle learned as he recovered from the illness that had nearly claimed his life. Doubtless he would have loved to lie down and give up, but the cost of the struggle had to be measured against the enormous potential revealed by his exploration. He had named Louisiana in honor of Louis XIV. Now he must see the king to persuade him to back up that claim with men, ships, and supplies.

6

New Directions

In 1683, La Salle was at the end of his rope financially. He had neither money nor credit available to him, but his spirit remained strong.

Headed for France

As he left the Illinois Country, La Salle met a canoe full of Frenchmen carrying orders from the new governor. La Barre had commissioned them to take possession of Fort Saint Louis. La Salle waved them on, sending a messenger of his own to Tonty, urging him to receive them well and follow their orders. This, doubtless, was one of the most difficult commands Tonty ever received.

La Salle paddled on, heading for Montreal and then Quebec. He had his first meeting with Governor la Barre early in the autumn of 1683, and was distressed to find him an unyielding foe. La Barre, won over by the Montreal merchants, was completely opposed to La Salle and to any further exploration in the Far West. There was nothing for them to do but to return to France to win a fair hearing.

Versailles

In the four years that had passed since La Salle was in France, Louis XIV had raised his court and the nation to an even higher level. In May 1682, just one month after La Salle reached the Mississippi's mouth, Louis XIV had made his new palace at Versailles the official seat of French government. Versailles had been a hunting lodge in the time of Louis XIII, then a favorite haunt of Louis XIV. It now became the center of the French court, and remained so until 1789, the year of the French Revolution.

La Salle did not go at once to Versailles, for he now knew the layers of bureaucracy and nepotism that existed at the court. It would do no good to appear suddenly and ask for assistance. Instead, he paved his way by staying in humble Parisian lodgings and spreading the word that he was eager to help the king make France even grander than she was already.

It is quite possible that La Salle would have languished for months—even years—before receiving a summons, but he now had two powerful allies: Abbott Claude Bernou and Eusebe Renaudot. These two churchmen, both members of the Sulpician Order, had long dreamed of establishing a larger, greater French empire in the New World. To do so at the expense of Spain and its king was their fondest hope.

Louis XIV and King Carlos II of Spain were distant relations, but that made little difference in the world of European diplomacy. France was on the way up, and Spain on the way down, so Louis was eager to plunder his royal relative of lands and fortune. France and Spain had exchanged declarations of war in 1682, but the contest had not heated up into a major war. Now, however, two churchmen allied themselves with La Salle and with a Spanish renegade.

In 1682, King Louis decided that the court and the seat of government would move from Paris to Versailles. Well-to-do French citizens flocked to Versailles in order to be close to the king and to power. Versailles featured 5,000 acres (20 sq km) of gardens, a 500-member kitchen staff, and housed at least 10,000 people.

The count of Penalosa had briefly been governor of New Spain. His headquarters had been at Mexico City, but his greatest New World interest was the silver mines of the province of New Biscay, now in the northern part of Mexico. The count had betrayed his fatherland, come to France, and now he proposed that Louis XIV use the war as a pretext for capturing the silver mines of New Biscay. The count was too old to lead the expedition himself and his two closest allies, the abbots, were churchmen and bound to pacifism. But they found a new friend in La Salle.

The Plan

In the winter of 1684, Louis XIV and the Marquis de Seignelay, minister of the navy, received a set of memorials from the two abbots. Some of the writing purported to be from La Salle, but most of it echoed of Old World interests and concepts rather than ones from America. To anyone who had ever spoken with the count of Penalosa, it was obvious that this new plan was but a variation of his old one, but the two abbots did their work well. They convinced La Salle to falsify the geography of the Mississippi, making it 250 leagues (1,207 km) to the west, meaning, closer to the mines of Mexico. They emphasized the importance of La Salle's discovery of the Mississippi's mouth and declared that he was just the man to lead an expedition to seize the Spanish silver mines.

La Salle would, doubtless, have preferred a more realistic goal, such as settling the mouth of the Mississippi, but to win any audience at court he had to go along with the rather wild dreams of the count and the two abbots. The proposal was as follows: La Salle would sail from France to the mouth of the Mississippi. There he would build a fort and make a settlement. He would gather an immense army of 15,000 Native Americans, and, with himself as their leader, march across what is now Texas and New Mexico to seize the silver mines.

All this could be accomplished at a minimum expense to the French crown, the abbots claimed. All they asked for was two royal ships and enough arms and ammunition for the settlement to be established.

Of all the many plans and schemes laid before Louis XIV, this was probably the wildest. Even to imagine bringing 15,000 Native Americans under one banner was absurd. To think they would tamely follow La Salle—or anyone else—across the plains of Texas and the deserts of New Mexico was beyond dreaming. It was madness

No one knew this better than La Salle. He had witnessed up close the terrible feuds and rivalries between tribes like the Iroquois and the Illinois. He knew the pride of Native American warriors and how unlikely they were to follow any chieftain, no matter how great. Yet La Salle went along with the plan, affixing his name to it. Perhaps it was a move of utter desperation, for he was now bankrupt beyond repair. Perhaps the long illness he suffered in the summer of 1682 had harmed his mental faculties. Whatever the cause, he agreed to be the leader of this quest.

Approval

Generally, Louis XIV did not give in to outlandish plans. What attracted him to this one was the lack of expense to the royal treasury. The abbots made it seem as if he would gain a fortune while risking very little. In May 1684, the king gave his royal assent and ordered La Salle to the port city of La Rochelle in western France to gather his ships, arms, and men. The king agreed to provide two ships and to find 100 sailors for each, but La Salle was charged with finding the balance of the sailors. This seemed, at the time, a worthwhile risk.

Even as Louis XIV approved the enterprise, he complicated it by splitting the command into two parts. La Salle was the overall commander of the entire project, but while at sea the ships were under the command of Captain Beaujeu, who was responsible for their safety. In his instructions to Beaujeu, the minister of the marine emphasized that La Salle had the top billing, but that Beaujeu could countermand him if he believed the ships (which the crown seemed to value more than the sailors) were in jeopardy.

Perhaps the minister of the marine believed that two Normans—one old and the other middle-aged—would get along well. If so, this was one of the biggest miscalculations of the entire plan.

Loggerheads

La Salle met Captain Beaujeu for the first time while they were still in Paris. They shared a dinner together and spoke of their mutual plans. La Salle made it seem as if Louis XIV was ready to commit more than was really the case, telling Beaujeu that other royal ships and forces would follow them in the next year or two. Perhaps La Salle said this to delude the captain, but more likely he was deluding himself. La Salle knew this would be a dangerous, even a desperate, endeavor. He hoped against likelihood that the king would furnish more troops and ammunition.

Beaujeu was puzzled by La Salle. Norman-born, the captain had spent almost 30 years in the king's navy. Most of his career had been noteworthy, but there had been a lapse in a recent campaign against the Algerian pirates, a lapse which led to the captain's confinement for several months. Just as La Salle wished to become a great success and to pay off his staggering debts, so did the captain desire to clear his name from the Algerian fiasco. Beaujeu also fretted that he would not be in France to apply for his pension.

La Salle and Beaujeu parted company, with Beaujeu headed straight for La Rochelle. La Salle remained in Paris for some weeks, hoping to make some improvement in his financial affairs. He did not succeed, but there was one consolation: While serving under the king's commission, he could not be harassed by his creditors.

La Belle

The king's commission called for two royal ships for La Salle, one a warship, and the other a *barque longue*, meaning a narrow ship which could be assembled or disassembled in order to be placed into another ship's hold. The warship was quickly found. She was the 36-gun *Le Joly*, and Captain Beaujeu raised his flag from her deck. But there was no barque longue handy, so the 50-foot (15-meter) *La Belle* (the *Bell*) was built from scratch in the La Rochelle dockyard. This could have caused a perilous delay, but remarkably she was ready at the time La Salle arrived in the port town.

Conflict

La Salle and Beaujeu were still on speaking terms, but they did not see eye-to-eye. Much worse, La Salle had to contend with the king's treasurer, who was determined to get everything for the least cost, and with other officials who wished to get out of the matter altogether.

This was a frustrating time for La Salle and many times his reactions went too far. Under strain from the ruin of his finances and desperately needing this expedition to be successful, he began to quarrel with almost everyone, including the younger brother of Henry de Tonty, who was along for the expedition.

La Salle kept no diary at this part of his life (at least not one that has survived) so most of the information about his conflicts comes from the writings of Beaujeu, who already had a negative view of the explorer. Many historians have given La Salle the benefit of the doubt, assuming the captain was an ill-humored man who should already have been on the retired list, but recent evidence suggests La Salle and Beaujeu were equally at fault. The captain wrote letters with friends, letters in which he criticized La Salle, and the explorer was much too prone to emotional outbursts. One of their worst confrontations happened when La Salle insisted that more men and barrels be brought aboard the *Joly*. The captain refused, the explorer demanded, and Beaujeu won the day, but at a price. Relations between the two men worsened.

Last Letter

Shortly before sailing from La Rochelle, La Salle wrote a letter to his mother, who still lived in his hometown of Rouen. Little of their correspondence survives, so this letter is an important indication both of their relationship and of his state of mind in 1684:

> Madame, My Most Honored Mother,
> At last, after having waited a long time for a favorable wind, and having had a great many difficulties to overcome, we are setting sail with four vessels, and nearly four hundred men on board. Everybody is well, including little Colin and my [other] nephew. We all have good hope of a happy success. We are not going by way of Canada, but by the Gulf of Mexico. I passionately wish, and so do we all, that the success of this voyage may contribute to your repose and comfort. Assuredly, I shall spare no effort that it may; and I beg you, on your part, to preserve yourself for the love of us.

It seems incredible that La Salle had not previously told his mother that the fleet was destined for the Gulf of Mexico. Perhaps he had neglected to inform her; perhaps he had concealed his hand to the very last minute, hoping that it might be possible to go the way he knew—the St. Lawrence River—rather than the one he did not.

The mention of "great many difficulties" was, if anything, an understatement, and the mention of his two nephews were significant, but not the whole story. Not only did he have two younger family members aboard, but his brother, Abbe Jean Cavelier, had shown up at the last minute and asked to be included. Given that Jean had helped himself, financially, at his brother's expense, it seems incredible that La Salle agreed to take him. Yet he did.

The four ships—the *Joly* (the warship), the *Belle* (the barque), *L'Aimable* (the storage ship), and the *Saint Francis* (the ketch, or long-distance cruiser), sailed from La Rochelle on July 20, 1684.

Seventeenth-Century Geography

Captain Beaujeu confessed his anxieties shortly before departure. He wrote to a friend that:

> I am going to an unknown country to seek something almost as hard to find as the philosopher's stone, late in the season…and with a troubled man.

Why was the Mississippi so hard to find?

Geographers were making great strides in the late seventeenth century, but some of their greatest contributions came just a year or two too late to assist La Salle and Captain Beaujeu. The English philosopher Isaac Newton's *Principia* was published in London that very year, 1684, and both the Royal Academy in London and the Academie de Francaises in Paris were working on the thorny problem of calculating longitude. Even so, La Salle sailed for the Mississippi using roughly the same type of tools and charts that Samuel de Champlain had employed 80 years before.

A False Start

La Salle's expedition sailed on July 24, but within four days it had to turn back. The *Joly*, flagship of the squadron, lost her bowsprit.

La Salle was, understandably, furious over the delay, but for once things were put right. The mast was replaced in record time and the squadron sailed again, on August 1, 1684.

Soon there was an altercation between La Salle and Beaujeu, with the latter wishing to stop at the Portuguese Madeira Islands, and the latter insisting the ships sail right on. Both men were right. Beaujeu was correct in wanting fresh water for his sailors, while La Salle was correct about the lateness of the season. If the ships did not reach the Caribbean soon, the men might well succumb to the autumn epidemic of yellow fever.

LATITUDE AND LONGITUDE

Latitude means one's distance from the equator, north or south, while longitude means one's distance from Greenwich, just east of London.

In La Salle's time, latitude had been reasonably well established. A captain took numerous sightings during the day, figuring his position relative to the North Star and to well-known marks at sea. Even so, latitude measurements were often off by as much as one degree, or 60 miles (96.5 km).

Longitude was much more difficult. In the first place, Greenwich Mean Time had not yet been established, so the sailors of different nations reckoned longitude from the capitals of their nations. Second, no one had yet figured a way for clocks to maintain one correct "time" while at sea; one fanciful projection was that cannon built on special platforms should fire at each hour on the hour!

La Salle was further handicapped in that even his reckoning of the Mississippi mouth's latitude was off. He had had only a faulty astrolabe while he canoed down the Father of Waters, leading his calculations to be off by as much as 100 miles (160.9 km). To perfect his miscalculations, there was a special error of observation. La Salle believed that the mouth of the Mississippi, where he had only spent two days, pointed east-by-southeast instead of due south. This meant he was looking for something, a river entry, that looked quite different from what he remembered.

Captain Beaujeu had not been far wrong in saying that finding the mouth of the great river was like finding the philosopher's stone.

Across the Atlantic

The squadron made reasonable time across the Atlantic, with the little ketch, the *Saint Francis*, continually lagging behind. There was an altercation when La Salle refused to allow the sailors to perform a traditional ceremony. When crossing the Tropic of Cancer, sailors often threatened to "initiate" passengers by keelhauling them (tying a sailor with rope and throwing him overboard on one side of the ship, then dragging him under the keel to the other side). Tradition had it that the passengers should make gifts of money to avoid the treatment. La Salle stopped the ceremony for this voyage, but, as one of the diarists commented, "They would gladly have killed us all."

La Salle and Beaujeu continued to feud as the voyage progressed. Sometimes their altercations had to do with small matters, but as they neared the coast of Saint-Domingue (present-day Haiti), the disagreements led to Beaujeu moving to the last, rather than the first, of all possible ports. This meant additional sailing for the weary passengers, but much worse it led to the *Saint Francis* being picked off by Spanish privateers. La Salle and his fleet staggered into the port, down from four ships to three.

La Salle fell gravely ill, so weak that he could not meet the civil authorities who came to greet him. Beaujeu should have taken on the role of greeting these men and informing them of the growing difficulties, but he maintained—perhaps accurately—that La Salle would be furious for any such interference. For days, then weeks, the expedition went without effective leadership. About 20 expedition members deserted, usually to the higher-paying privateer ships in the harbor. When La Salle recovered his health, he recruited new men from the port, usually ending up with renegades and desperadoes.

Into the Spanish Sea

At least the Atlantic Ocean was largely known. The same could not be said of the Gulf of Mexico which had been a Spanish sea for more than 100 years. La Salle knew that the Armada of the West, as the Spanish termed their defensive fleet, was well armed and dangerous, but he simply had to proceed. To turn back now would mean complete ruin—financial, moral, and otherwise. There is every reason to expect he would have been confined to the Bastille had he returned to France with nothing to show for his efforts.

Beaujeu was wary of the Gulf of Mexico because he had no native pilot. La Salle had concealed the expedition's true designs so well that even the chief naval captain had not had time to gain knowledge of the tides and seasons of the Gulf of Mexico. From the pirate and privateer captains of Saint-Domingue, Beaujeu learned that the Gulf of Mexico was treacherous: one could be surprised by sudden changes in the wind that could drive vessels upon the rocks of the northwestern shore, in what is now Texas.

All the difficulties and hazards notwithstanding, La Salle and Beaujeu set sail in November 1684, headed for the mouth of the Mississippi.

Legends versus Reality

La Salle had, of course, seen the Mississippi's mouth just two and a half years before, but he had seen it from the northern, or coastal side. Also, he had spent only two days in the vicinity. Therefore, as the expedition sailed through the Gulf of Mexico, he was not sure what to look for.

La Salle fell victim both to his own self assurance and to the changing nature of Louisiana geography. The mouth of the great river looked different, just two years after he had seen it, and he had no notion of just how far to sail. To avoid mistakes, La Salle directed Beaujeu to sail far to the northwest, thinking that the Mississippi flowed into the Gulf of Mexico far beyond where it did. Based on journals and the ship's log, it is estimated that the squadron sailed too far off the coast to see the mouth.

With Spain and France at war, La Salle was charged with establishing a colony on the Mississippi that would serve as a base to strike at Mexico. This would deter Spanish shipping and block English expansion, while providing a warm water port for the Mississippi valley fur trade. After experiencing much misfortune, La Salle and others finally landed at Matagorda Bay in Texas.

Even if it had, it is likely they would have missed it, disguised behind immense conglomerations of logs, mud, and rock.

So it was that the squadron wound up 300 miles (482.8 km) west of the Father of Waters, in what is today coastal Texas rather than the bayous of Louisiana.

Coming Ashore

La Salle and the first of his men disembarked around January 15, 1687. They came ashore near the site of present-day Galveston, Texas. Protected by a lagoon (a sea wall was added in the

THE TALON FAMILY

One of the most poignant stories from the attempted settlement of Louisiana belongs to a Canadian family that had been persuaded the southern shores were better than the northern ones.

Lucien and Isabelle Talon were French-Canadians, born and bred just outside Quebec City. Marrying in 1672, they had five children and were living the typical hard but healthy life of Canadian farmers when they learned of La Salle's discovery of the Mississippi in 1682. Husband and wife made the decision to go all the way to France, visit relatives, and then embark with La Salle and Beaujeu in the summer of 1684. During their brief time in France, the Talons had their sixth child, a daughter.

Embarking on the Louisiana expedition, the Talons experienced the difficulties and trials of the ocean voyage, but they had one great consolation: a son who was born at sea. La Salle gave his name to Robert Talon and became godfather to the boy, who, everyone expected would be ennobled by Louis XIV as the first-born child of a new colony.

twentieth century), this region seemed close enough to where the Mississippi should be. Once ashore, La Salle should have realized that the coastal sands and scrub brush were quite unlike what he had known in Louisiana. But he was unable to see his mistake, or perhaps to admit to it.

Beaujeu kept the three ships—the *Joly, Aimable,* and *Belle*—about 3 miles (4.8 km) offshore to avoid sudden wind changes that might strip them of their anchors. As a result, it took almost a week for all the men to disembark. Even then there were controversies over the cannon, cannon balls, and blocks of iron. La Salle rightly claimed that all these belonged to him and the colony, but Beaujeu needed them, the blocks of iron most especially, to keep the proper balance in his ships' holds.

La Salle and Beaujeu actually got along better at this point than before. The naval captain, seeing how desperate the situation was, offered to sail to Martinique and bring back more men and supplies. La Salle, for his part, seemed unwilling to admit how very wrong things had gone. He stuck to his belief that Galveston Bay was an offshoot of the Mississippi River, which he would soon find.

He could not have been more wrong.

Disasters

The *Aimable* went aground on a sand bar in March 1685. One sudden turn of the wind, and a lax state of affairs aboard, turned her into a sinking wreck. La Salle and Beaujeu had the better part of a week to empty her hold—which was accomplished— but her fate cast a dismal pall over the entire expedition. The king's engineer, intended to build La Salle's fort, refused to come ashore. Whether this was because of stubborness or because of continued conflicts with La Salle is difficult to say. La Salle now began to act like something of a mad man. Irritated by the mountain of details, upset by his inability to find the

Mississippi, La Salle actually seemed eager to dismiss Beaujeu and send away the *Joly*.

Beaujeu remained until the beginning of spring. He sent a stream of letters asking to be of assistance, but La Salle waved him off. There was no way, he wrote, to ensure that the civil authorities at Martinique would help. Beaujeu should sail for France and inform the minister of the colonies of the situation. La Salle sent a series of his own dispatches, which indicate he was unable to face the difficulties of the situation. He continued to act as if he had found the Mississippi, and that it was only a matter of time before he established a lasting settlement.

Catastrophe

Given the long series of conflicts between La Salle and Captain Beaujeu, one might think that the latter sailing off was a blessing for La Salle and his settlers. Yet things were about to become even worse.

Fort Saint Louis

In the spring of 1685, La Salle and his colonists started building what they called Fort Saint Louis (it had the same name as the fort in the Illinois Country). They started the building a few miles inland to keep away from the eyes of Spanish ships.

The enterprise was difficult from the beginning. The engineer of the expedition had sailed off with Beaujeu aboard the *Joly*, and though the colonists had plenty of nails and hammers, they lacked a good supply of wood. It is easy to criticize La Salle's choice of location, but wherever he went, for about 50 miles (80 km) in either direction, the landscape looked much the same.

Established roughly 40 miles (60 km) inland from where La Salle and the settlers landed, Fort St. Louis was the first European settlement on the Gulf Coast. The fort was intended to serve only as a temporary outpost while La Salle continued searching for the Mississippi. These eight cannon had been arranged around a crude dwelling but offered no defense since there were no cannonballs of the right caliber. They were found during an archaeological dig in 1996 by the Texas Historical Commission.

The colonists showed signs of splitting into different factions, or groups. A hard-core group of perhaps 20 were strongly loyal to La Salle and his mission, but at least three times that number doubted both the leader and his plans. Still another group composed of men who had come aboard in Saint-Domingue were dead-set against La Salle and did their best to undermine his authority.

In the winter of 1685, La Salle decided to head off to look for the Mississippi, which he still believed lay west of Fort Saint Louis. La Salle left Henri Joutel, his most trusted lieutenant, in charge of the fort and headed north and west, looking for the river.

Joutel had kept a diary from the beginning of the voyage, but his entries now took on a more urgent tone. He was in charge, and it was up to him to see that the settlers did not starve. There were some comic moments, such as when the Frenchmen engaged in their first buffalo hunt. Though surrounded by nearly 6,000 beasts, they did not bring down a single one that day, and it took some weeks before they became proficient in the hunting, skinning, and roasting of buffalo. Father Membre, who had been with La Salle in the Illinois Country and on the trip down the Mississippi in 1682, now got into trouble. Poking a buffalo he believed dead, the Jesuit was stunned when the animal reared up and attacked him. Father Membre took some bad wounds and was laid up for over a month.

Then there were difficulties with the Native Americans. Joutel described it in his diary:

> I commanded all our people to be on guard. I enforced this without exception and gave no pardon to those who fell asleep while on sentry duty. This made them realize that our survival depended on that.

Joutel was a hard master. He punished and threatened the offenders so much that the men from Saint-Domingue began to collect supporters, even from among La Salle's original loyalists. Had La Salle not returned in the spring of 1686, complete chaos might have resulted.

Fresh Hopes

La Salle came back, having gone at least 200 miles (321.8 km) in a northwest direction. Nothing he saw reminded him of the Mississippi landscape from 1682. Instead, it seemed only to pull him farther and farther away from his goal. He met few Native Americans on this journey, but he did return with some horses, the first his colonists had seen since leaving France. They may have been runaways from the Spanish settlements

UNDERWATER ARCHAEOLOGY

Nineteen eighty-five was a banner year for the burgeoning new field of nautical archaeology. On July 20, members of the Mel Fisher family located the wreck of the Spanish treasure galleon *Atocha*, which had lain beneath the sea since 1715. On September 1, Robert Ballard and a team of American scientists based at Woods Hole Oceanographic Institute on Cape Cod located the wreck of R.M.S. *Titanic,* which had sunk in April 1912. Ballard followed this with an equally sensational discovery. He found the wreck of battleship *Bismarck* in June 1989.

Underwater archaeology has been with us for centuries. Spaniards of the seventeenth century often used primitive equipment looking for their own lost treasure ships. But the field came into its own shortly after the Second World War, which, with its use of radar and sonar, had opened the way for new discoveries.

The *Atocha* proved to be the single richest find by American underwater archaeologists. The Fisher family created a private in New Mexico. Furnished with horses, La Salle now hoped to make another journey, this time to the northeast. But he had to reckon with one more, painful loss.

The *Belle* wrecked in the winter of 1685–1686. Her captain had shown himself to be negligent and a drunk several times, but La Salle had kept him in command. The little bark was brought into Galveston Bay, where she did good service for some months, but in a winter storm she dragged her anchor and was wrecked in shoal water. Aboard were La Salle's papers, his navigational instruments, and whatever money was meant to purchase supplies for the colonists. A bad situation had suddenly become a desperate one.

museum in Key West, Florida, where tourists can handle gold, silver, and pieces of eight (all safely locked or tied to the museum wall). The discovery of the *Titanic* spawned a whole new industry, leading to more nautical searches and helping to inspire artistic creations such as the film of the same name, which debuted in 1997. But there were other, less sensational, discoveries which helped further the cause of knowledge.

In December 1994, a French-Canadian diver, who had spent years looking for old French shipwrecks, found an English one almost in his backyard (it was the *Elizabeth and Mary*, built in Boston, which had sunk on her way back from a campaign against Quebec). In July 1995, members of the Texas Historical Commission found the wreck of the *Belle*, so far the oldest French shipwreck found in the New World. There have also been finds of pirate shipwrecks, most notably the *Whydah*, which sank off the extreme end of Cape Cod in 1717.

It is little wonder that the years since 1985 are seen as a new golden age of archaeology. Many great finds have been made, but, given the high number of ships that sank in the oceans of the world, it is likely that many more remain undiscovered.

The Second Journey

In April 1686, La Salle set off a second time, this time in the direction of what is now Arkansas. He had little sense of where he was going, only a desperate sense that he must find the Mississippi and bring his colonists to its mouth. The once-exciting idea of attacking the Spanish silver mines had vanished from the realm of possibility.

Joutel again commanded the survivors at Fort Saint Louis, who became increasingly unruly. He had his hands full with basic survival, commenting that "In the end, only our husbandry [farming] mattered." In addition, there continued to be conflicts within the settlement, with not one but three mothers claiming possible titles of nobility for their infants.

Pierre and Catherine Talon had a son that was born on the naval voyage. They claimed that he should receive ennoblement from Louis XIV. A high-born member of the expedition, the Marquis of La Sablonniere, wed a young girl from Paris in 1686. They claimed that their son, although he had been still-born, should receive the honor. Then there was still a third family claiming the privilege.

Joutel probably saw all of this social wrangling as a complete waste of time, but there were times when he probably wished for a diversion of any kind. Luckily, La Salle returned in August, with a mixture of good and bad news.

La Salle had not found the Mississippi, but he believed he was now on the right track. He had spent some weeks with the Cenis, a Native American group in the central part of present-day Texas. La Salle would have starved had Nika, a friendly Shawnee, not provided meat.

La Salle now put the matter squarely to Joutel: "[He] asked me one day if I would be inclined to take this journey, to go to Canada afterwards, and from there to France to bring back a ship, for I had some knowledge [of navigation]."

A taller order could hardly have been made. La Salle asked Joutel to go north, find the Mississippi, trace it to the Illinois and then to the Great Lakes, to reach Canada and finally France. It was a journey that would have made Joutel one of the best-traveled men of his time.

Joutel said he was agreeable to whatever La Salle wished, but the explorer soon realized that he needed to go as well. Only he had seen the length of the Mississippi and knew the canoe approaches to the Great Lakes. On January 12, 1687, La Salle, his brother Jean, Joutel, and about 20 others left Fort Saint Louis. They had a handful of horses to carry most of the baggage, and they had enough powder and ball for hunting, but they made a sorry sight as they left. As for the 100-odd settlers of Fort Saint-Louis, some of them were in even worse shape.

Third and Last

No diary of La Salle's survives from this time period, but we imagine him torn and conflicted as he led his men northeast. He had brought them to this state, and only he could get them out.

He had no compass, no instruments, and no reliable maps. His own navigational ability—so prominent during 1682—had failed him in 1684 and 1685. Yet he continued on.

La Salle had one great hope remaining. Of all the men who had served him over the years, only three had been outstandingly loyal. One was Nika, the Shawnee. Another was Joutel, and the third was Henry de Tonty, still commanded Fort Saint Louis in the Illinois Country. La Salle had no way of getting a message to Tonty, but he hoped against hope that Tonty would come south in search of him and his colonists.

The explorers met Native Americans as they traveled, and on each meeting La Salle told them he was going to spend time with the Cenis to the north. This kept them out of trouble with the Native Americans. Nika proved his usual capable self when it came to buffalo hunting, and the men were well supplied with meat, but they had no bread, almost nothing to provide the quick energy that comes from carbohydrates. They met with a Cenis hunting group, and then progressed across the Brazos River in central Texas. Had they known how far they were from their goal—either the mouth of the Mississippi or the Illinois Country—they might have given up from despair. Still, La Salle kept them going.

La Salle felt the desperation of some of the men. One, known simply as L'Archeveque, was quietly planning a mutiny. La Salle had, time and again, proven himself able to quell such uprisings, but L'Archeveque and his conspirators struck on the morning of March 19, 1687. Joutel later described the scene:

> La Salle, on leaving, had directed me to make smoke sig-
> nals from hour to hour by setting fire to the small area of
> dry grass on a rise....toward evening I was greatly sur-
> prised, as I was going to the rise, to see one of the men ap-
> proaching who had left with the first group to collect the
> corn. When we met, I saw that he was quite stupefied and
> rather wandering. On approaching me, he began to tell
> me that there was news and that a mishap had occurred. I
> asked him what. He told me that La Salle was dead, and so
> was Morenger and two others, the Indian [Nika] and the
> gentleman's servant [Saget].

Joutel was dumbfounded. Soon, he was confronted by L'Archeveque and the others who claimed responsibility, and some pride, for the deed. They had lured La Salle into hunting geese and shot him where he stood in the high grass. They had stripped his body and left it for the wolves.

Joutel doubtless would have liked to strike the murderers with his fists, but they had guns and he did not. In addition, Abbe Jean Cavelier, La Salle's brother, appeared, saying that

By 1687, the original 320 people had been reduced to 36. The men were frustrated and angered by La Salle's ill temper and aimless two-year search for the Mississippi River. On March 19, 1687, Pierre Duhault and his companions ambushed La Salle, shot him, divided his possessions, and left his body for the wolves.

vengeance must be left to God. So the murderers and the loyalists spent the next several weeks in each other's company.

At first, Joutel and Abbe Cavelier hoped to be rid of the assassins, who spoke of going back to Fort Saint Louis. But, as it became obvious that the only way was forward, the entire party made its way north, reaching the Mississippi River in the vicinity of the Arkansas Indian villages, where Marquette and Joliet had been a decade and a half earlier. From there it was straight north, and on to the Illinois River, and eventually to the other Fort Saint Louis, commanded by Henry de Tonty.

Tonty had again proven faithful. Learning that La Salle had sailed from France to found a Mississippi valley colony, Tonty had gone south in 1686, searching everywhere for his mentor and friend. Tonty had followed the Mississippi River all the way to its opening to the Gulf of Mexico, then returned. Now, in the summer of 1687, he entertained the handful of survivors, who did not tell him the truth.

Perhaps it was the conspirators who "fixed" the conversation. It may also have been Abbe Cavelier. For whatever reason, the seven men who arrived at Fort Saint Louis in Illinois County told Tonty that La Salle was alive and well, and that there was indeed a colony in the south, though not on the Mississippi itself. This deception would lead Tonty to undertake yet another journey, one of complete frustration.

Abbe Cavelier and Joutel lived to reach France. Soon, the news spread of La Salle's assassination. Charges were soon to follow.

La Salle
and the West:
His Legacy

Louis XIV and the Marquis de Seignelay were completely ignorant of what had happened in Texas. The first news the French court had was in the summer of 1686, when Captain Beaujeu sailed the *Joly* back to La Rochelle.

Those Who Returned

Beaujeu submitted a massive list of documents and letters, most of which indicated that he was the saner of the two men. They indicated that La Salle had led his colonists on a madman's journey of exploration. Even so, Beaujeu did care about the colonists, so he urged the king and minister to send men and supplies to Texas.

Louis XIV was displeased with Beaujeu, but more incensed with the engineer who had chosen to return aboard the *Joly* rather than build a fort in America. The engineer was confined to the tower at La Rochelle for some months before being reinstated.

The Marquis de Seignelay showed little concern for the colonists in Texas. The records and investigations indicate that he, like the king, was much more concerned with the crown's financial investment. Had France and Spain still been at war, Louis XIV might have wished to do something for these forsaken folk, but the two countries had actually come to peace terms not long after La Salle and Beaujeu had sailed, back in 1684. Louis XIV wished to keep the new peace with Spain; therefore, he did not send ships, money, or men into the Gulf of Mexico.

For their part, the Spanish were indeed active. Historian William C. Foster, who studied the Spanish record closely, declared that La Salle's intended settlement had the inadvertent result of launching a second phase of Spanish exploration in the Gulf of Mexico and along the coast of Texas. No fewer than five Spanish groups—three by sea and two by land—went in search of La Salle between 1687 and 1691. One group found the sad remains of what had been the second Fort Saint Louis.

Corpses abounded, as did wreckage, but there was no one living at the place. The Spaniards continued to investigate. Eventually they found several survivors, all of them living with the Native Americans. One Frenchman, known simply as "Garry," had lived with one group for over a year, persuading them that he was some kind of living god. Three of the Talon brothers, ranging between 12 and 16, were also found. The brothers had been taken by the Spaniards to Mexico City, where they served as household servants to the viceroy.

The Talon brothers went on to have a remarkable life. After several years in Mexico, they shipped out for Spain aboard a treasure ship, only to be captured by a French privateer and returned to their motherland. There, they were interrogated at length, providing one of the most detailed stories of the sad end of Fort Saint Louis.

The Native Americans had intruded all the while, and the settlers eventually ran out of food. Muskets became useless from rust and nails were of no use when there was no wood. The colonists lost heart and fell victim to disease, accident, and even suicide. The Talon brothers had been able to escape, but nearly everyone else had died.

Is it any wonder that Louis XIV and the Marquis of Seignelay considered this an unmitigated disaster?

A Decade of War

England, Holland, Germany, and Spain all went to war against France in 1689, starting what Europeans call the Nine Years War, and which Americans usually call King William's War, in honor of William III of England. The war involved the Five Nations of Iroquois (who sided with the English) and the Abenaki and Illinois tribes (who sided with the French), but the lower Mississippi valley saw no outbursts of warfare. The Native Americans there were hardly aware of England or France, Holland, or Spain. But as the great war came to an end, in 1697, Louis XIV decided to take action in America.

Pierre Le Moyne d'Iberville, a French-Canadian born in Montreal, was then in Paris, asking for permission to do something against the English in America. Iberville had already proven himself a resourceful ship captain and forest fighter. Louis XIV did not wish to resume the contest with the English and their Dutch allies, but it made sense to follow up on what La Salle had begun.

Making the matter more urgent, Father Louis Hennepin came out with a new edition of his book. Not only did he describe Niagara Falls and the Illinois Country in detail, but he dedicated the book to King William of England, suggesting that Englishmen, rather than Frenchmen, should populate the Mississippi River valley. That idea was intolerable to Louis XIV, who commissioned Pierre d'Iberville to sail to Louisiana.

Pierre le Moyne d'Iberville was regarded as one of the most skillful naval officers in the French service. In 1698, he was chosen to lead an expedition to rediscover the mouth of the Mississippi River and to colonize Louisiana, which the English also wanted. Over the next five years, Iberville continued his southern exploits, with occasional trips back to France. In 1703, he was named the first governor of Louisiana.

Up the Mississippi

Iberville had much better luck than La Salle. He sailed later in the year and avoided both the Caribbean hurricanes and the dreaded yellow fever. Iberville knew, from La Salle's experience, that the mouth of the Mississippi was located more to the east. He coasted along the Louisiana shore till he found a powerful river, whose mouth was blocked by large sections of dirt, stone, and collected logs (Iberville called it the Bird-foot Delta). Breaking through this natural barricade, Iberville sailed north. Within hours he was certain that he had found La Salle's Mississippi, the first man to do so from the ocean side. Iberville went as far north as present-day Baton Rouge, Louisiana, which he named for a red stick that was on the side of the river.

Iberville did not truly colonize on this voyage. That was left to subsequent expeditions. But he laid the basis for what became the French colony of Louisiana.

Henry de Tonty came down the Mississippi and joined Iberville in 1699. Tonty was a mainstay of the fledgling colony until his death in Mobile, Alabama, in 1702.

La Salle's Legacy

Historians are of many minds about La Salle. Some, especially those who wrote in the early twentieth century, consider him one of the great explorers of all time. Others, especially those who wrote in the 1990s, think of him as a brilliant but misguided man who led his followers into one disaster after another.

Francis Parkman, whose *La Salle and the Discovery of the Great West* was published in 1893, believed La Salle to be the most indomitable of all explorers. True, La Salle did come back from many failures and reverses, some of which would have frightened off a weaker person.

FRENCH LOUISIANA

La Salle was the first explorer to canoe to the Mississippi's mouth, and Iberville was the first sailor to come into the Father of Waters from its coastal entrance. Both men deserve credit for the founding of French Louisiana.

Iberville first came in 1699. He returned to France that same year, leaving behind his younger brother, Jean-Baptiste Le Moyne d'Bienville, to guard the tiny settlement. Bienville became the guardian spirit of Louisiana, founding New Orleans in 1718, and serving as governor of the colony over many years (Iberville died in the Caribbean in 1706).

French Louisiana remained small in population. The French people seemed no more eager to come to the swampy bayous and heat of Louisiana than to the cold and frosts of Canada. But New Orleans, situated right on the Mississippi, had potential as a merchant town, and the French kept control of it until 1762. In that year, France ceded Louisiana to Spain, rather than risk losing it to the British in the Seven Years War.

Spain kept Louisiana for the next 38 years, then gave it back to France in 1800. This move was forced by Napoleon Bonaparte, then the First Consul of France. Napoleon nursed dreams of a second French empire in America, but, like La Salle, his dreams were hampered by disease and death. A French army sent to subdue Haiti was torn to bits by the enemy and by yellow fever. Napoleon reluctantly gave up on his idea, selling the entire Louisiana Territory to the United States in 1803.

Robert S. Weddle, who spent many years researching La Salle, believed that La Salle's greatest triumph was the building of the *Griffin*, for it launched the age of ocean-going ships on the Great Lakes. Weddle came to the conclusion that La Salle was a deeply flawed man, one who would never listen to the advice of others (this charge was also levied during his own lifetime, by writers such as Father Hennepin).

The only way to evaluate La Salle's skill, or lack thereof, is to compare him with explorers of his own time. In that comparison, he does not fare badly.

Samuel de Champlain, the Frenchman who founded Quebec in 1608, went almost as far as La Salle and cleared the path for subsequent French explorers. Champlain never experienced shipwreck and total loss, as La Salle did in Texas.

Henry Hudson, the Englishman who pioneered in Hudson's Bay, was set adrift by his own men, stranded in a manner that reminds one of La Salle's own tragic end. English explorers, like Henry Woodward of South Carolina, covered almost as much ground as La Salle, but they did not take to the waterways as he did, so it is difficult to make a useful comparison.

This much is certain: La Salle pointed the way toward the American heartland, the vast space between the Great Lakes and the Gulf of Mexico, and the Appalachian and Rocky Mountains. He did not live to enjoy his own success, but we can still applaud his mighty efforts.

CHRONOLOGY

1643   Robert de La Salle is born in Rouen, Normandy,
        France, on November 22.

1667   La Salle leaves the Jesuits (the Society of Jesus)
        to seek adventure. La Salle arrives in New France
        (Canada), where his brother Jean, a Sulpician
        priest, had moved the year before.

1668   La Salle is granted the fief of La Chine (in present-
        day Montreal).

1669   La Salle sails to the Lower Great Lakes.

TIMELINE

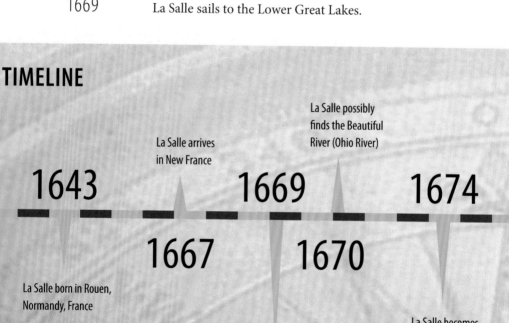

La Salle arrives in New France

La Salle possibly finds the Beautiful River (Ohio River)

1643   **1669**   **1674**

1667   **1670**

La Salle born in Rouen, Normandy, France

La Salle becomes commander of Fort Frontenac

La Salle goes to the Lower Great Lakes

1670	Few records of La Salle's actions during this time; theories say that he found the Beautiful River (Ohio River).
1672	Count Louis de Frontenac arrives in New France as governor-general. He establishes several forts on the Great Lakes.
1673	Father Marquette and Louis Joliet find the Mississippi River. Fort Frontenac is built in what is now Kingston, Ontario.
1674	La Salle becomes commander of Fort Frontenac.
1678	La Salle meets Italian fur trader Henry de Tonty in Paris. They become partners in exploration. La Salle and Tonty arrive in New France. Tonty is placed in charge of several French forts.
1679	La Salle sets sail on the *Griffin*. He and his crew sail up Lake Erie all the way to Green Bay, Wisconsin.

La Salle and Tonty arrive in New France. Tonty is placed in charge of several French forts

APRIL La Salle and Tonty reach mouth of the Mississippi River

La Salle is killed by three colonists

1681

1686

1678

1682

1687

1681–1682
La Salle and Tonty use the Chicago Portage

La Salle sets up third Fort Saint Louis in Texas. He leads the colonists on three expeditions to find Mississippi River

1680   Fort Crevecouer is built in what is now Peoria, Illinois.

1681   First Fort Saint Louis is built near present-day Ottawa, Illinois.

1681–1682   La Salle and Tonty use the Chicago Portage.

1682   APRIL   La Salle and Tonty reach the mouth of the Mississippi River. La Salle claims the Mississippi basin for France and calls it La Louisiane after King Louis XIV.

            NOVEMBER   Count Frontenac loses his governorship and is recalled to France after arguing with colony officials.

1683   La Salle sails for France for supplies. On the return voyage, he establishes the second Fort Saint Louis, on the Illinois River. Tonty is left in charge of the fort during La Salle's absence.

1684   APRIL   King Louis XIV approves the Louisiana plan to establish a French colony on the Gulf of Mexico, at the mouth of the Mississippi River. Their goal is for France to control the fur trade.

            JULY   La Salle sails from La Rochelle, France, with four ships and 300 colonists.

1685–1686   The expedition is plagued by pirates and hostile Native Americans. La Salle is unable to recall where he landed at the mouth of the Mississippi River two years earlier and gets them lost. One ship is lost to pirates in the West Indies. Another sinks in Matagorda Bay, on the Texas coast. A third runs aground.

1686   La Salle and the remaining colonists set up Fort Saint Louis of Texas, near present-day Victoria, Texas. He leads them on three expeditions on foot to try to find the Mississippi River.

1687   Three frustrated colonists mutiny near the site of
            modern Navasota, Texas. La Salle is killed and his
            body is left to the wolves.

1697–1699   King Louis XIV gives command to French soldier
            Pierre le Moyne d'Iberville to establish a colony at
            the mouth of the Mississippi River. He discovers
            the area known as Bixoli, Mississippi, and founds
            the French colony of Louisiana.

GLOSSARY

Black Robe (Black Gown)   name that Native Americans gave to French priests

Calumet   the pipe of peace and the ceremony that accompanied it

Cobbler   maker of shoes

Coffer-dam   man-made construction that allows water to be pumped out so that work can be done in a restricted area

Confluence   meeting place of two rivers or river systems

Illinois Country   corresponds roughly to what are now Ohio, Indiana, and Illinois

Illinois Tribe   lived in what are now Indiana and Illinois

Iroquois (Five Nations of)   lived in what is now upstate New York

Jesuits   members of the Society of Jesus, founded by Ignatius of Loyola in 1534

La Rochelle   a port on the southwest coast in France

Louisiana   named for King Louis XIV, in 1682

Marine (Minister of)   the French minister of the marine was responsible both for the Navy and the American colonies

Natchez   Native American tribe in what is now Louisiana and Mississippi

Norman   comes from "North-man's land." Refers to citizen of that province

NORMANDY   province in northwestern France

PORTAGE   carrying canoes or boats over a section of land between two bodies of water

SULPICIANS   members of the Order of Saint Sulpice

TONTINE   a devious form of life insurance named for Lorenzo de Tonty, father of La Salle's right-hand man

VERSAILLES   home of the French kings between 1682 and 1789

BIBLIOGRAPHY

Bass, George F., et al. *Beneath the Seven Seas: Adventures with the Institute of Nautical Archeology.* London: Thames and Hudson, 2005.

Donnelly, Joseph P., S.J. *Jacques Marquette, S.J.: 1637–1675.* Chicago: Loyola University Press, 1985.

Eccles, W.J. *The Canadian Frontier, 1534-1760.* Albuquerque: University of New Mexico Press, 1974.

Galloway, Patricia K. editor. *La Salle and his Legacy: Frenchmen and Indians in the Lower Mississippi Valley.* Jackson: University Press of Mississippi, 1982.

Lockridge, Ross F. *La Salle.* Yonkers-on-Hudson, N.Y.: World Book Company, 1931.

Murphy, Edmund Robert. *Henry De Tonty: Fur Trader of the Mississippi.* Washington, D.C.: Johns Hopkins University Press, 1941.

Parkman, Francis. *La Salle and the Discovery of the Great West.* New York: The Modern Library, 1999.

Weddle, Robert S. *The Wreck of the Belle, The Ruin of La Salle.* College Station: Texas A&M University Press, 2001.

FURTHER RESOURCES

Crompton, Samuel Willard. *100 Colonial Leaders who Shaped North America*. San Mateo, CA: Bluewood Books, 1999.

Fernandez-Armesto, Felipe. *Pathfinders: A Global History of Exploration*. New York: W.W. Norton, 2006.

Parkman, Francis. *La Salle and the Discovery of the Great West*. New York: The Modern Library, 1999.

WEB SITES

Catholic Encyclopedia: Father Louis Hennepin, Pierre Le Moyne d'Iberville
http://www.newadvent.org/cathen/07215c.htm
Biographical information about two of the most famous explorers of North America.

Fort Crevecoeur Park
http://ftcrevecoeur.org/
The site for the privately owned park, former location of the fort built by La Salle to defend the Peoria Indians against the Iroquois. The non-profit organization is dedicated to the education and preservation of the French heritage in central Illinois.

PBS, NOVA: "Voyage of Doom"
http://www.pbs.org/wgbh/nova/lasalle/
Companion Web site to the NOVA program "Voyage of Doom." The program reports on the discovery and excavation of the Belle. Includes activities for students and resources for teachers.

Starved Rock State Park
http://starvedrockstatepark.org/index.cfm?pageID=140
A site for travelers who wish to visit Starved Rock State Park along the Illinois River. This was the site where La Salle established the second Fort Saint Louis.

Texas Beyond History: The *Belle*

http://www.texasbeyondhistory.net/belle/

This site has detailed history and present-day information about the Belle, La Salle's ship that ran aground off the Texas coast. Includes maps, photographs of the excavation led by the Texas Historical Commission, and activities for students and teachers.

Texas Historical Commission: La Salle Shipwreck Project

http://www.thc.state.tx.us/aboutus/abtdefault.shtml

A detailed site about one of the most important shipwrecks ever discovered in North America. The site is supported by the state agency for historic preservation, the Texas Historical Commission.

PICTURE CREDITS

INDEX

ABOUT
THE AUTHOR

SAMUEL WILLARD CROMPTON is the author or editor of many books, including a number written for Chelsea House. A part-time professor of history at Westfield State College and Holyoke Community College, he was a member of the National Endowment for the Humanities group "French Travel Writing from the Americas" in 2003. Crompton is also a major contributor to the 24-volume *American National Biography*, published in 1999. He lives and works in the scenic Berkshire Hills of western Massachusetts.